Rosemary Verey's English Country Gardens

HENRY HOLT AND COMPANY

NEW YORK

ACKNOWLEDGEMENTS

I have many friends to thank for their help in the making of this book, based on the television series *The English Country Garden*.

Nicky Copeland at BBC Books has worked wonders with my text, putting together each seasonal piece and, with the help of Harry Green, the designer, has woven Andrew Lawson's and Jerry Harpur's pictures into each chapter.

I thank the garden owners and their head gardeners who are natural film stars and made me more aware of the importance of the flexibility of our English country style.

I thank David Bill, the executive producer—it was his idea for the series—Michael Attwell, who commissioned the series for BBC2, and Peter Murphy with his flair for original productions.

I thank all the television crew who were part of my life for the year and during that time became my friends. Keith Shearer was the director; Janet Ogilvie, the production manager; Graham Smith, the cameraman; Bernice Parker, his assistant; and Kevin Meredith quietly took care of the sounds in the gardens. They taught me so much—to appreciate in nature and in gardens, mine and other peoples'.

I WOULD LIKE TO THANK THE OWNERS OF THE FOLLOWING GARDENS FOR THEIR

CO-OPERATION AND HELP IN CREATING *THE ENGLISH COUNTRY GARDEN*

AND THE TELEVISION SERIES IT ACCOMPANIES. PLANS OF TEN OF THE GARDENS

ARE SHOWN AT THE END OF THE BOOK, TOGETHER WITH INFORMATION

ABOUT WHEN THEY CAN BE SEEN BY THE PUBLIC.

BARNSLEY HOUSE

Barnsley

Gloucestershire

Rosemary Verey, Charles Verey

Head gardener: Nick Burton

FOLLY FARM

Sulhamstead

Berkshire

The Hon. Hugh and Mrs Astor

Head gardener: Mr Honour

HOLKER HALL

Cark-in-Cartmel

Cumbria

Lord and Lady Cavendish

Head gardener: Graham Moulstone

BENINGTON LORDSHIP

Benington

Hertfordshire

Mr and Mrs C. H. A. Bott

Gardener: Richard Webb

GREAT DIXTER

Northiam

East Sussex

Christopher Lloyd

Head gardener: Fergus Garrett

KIFTSGATE COURT

Chipping Campden

Gloucestershire

Mr and Mrs J. G. Chambers

BLEDLOW MANOR

Bledlow

Buckinghamshire

Lord and Lady Carrington

Head gardener: Frank Bailey

THE GROVE

Brightwell Baldwin

Oxfordshire

Mr David and Lady Pamela Hicks

Gardeners: Paul Ballard, Peter Church

WINFIELD HOUSE

Regent's Park

London

Residence of the American Ambassador to the Court of St James's.

Head gardener: Stephen Crisp

CHILCOMBE HOUSE

Chilcombe

Dorset

Mr and Mrs J. Hubbard

Gardener: Malcolm Seal

HELMINGHAM HALL

Helmingham

Suffolk

Lord and Lady Tollemache

Head gardener: Roy Balaam

WOODSIDE

Berkshire

Elton John

Head gardener: Helen Finch

CONTENTS

AUTUMN

WINTER

INTRODUCTION

$\mathcal{E}$nglish country gardens are an integral part of our heritage and way of life. This book describes twelve outstanding gardens that I visited at different times of the year. There are many more that are equally beautiful and in making my choice I considered the typical characteristics of our gardens, old and young – good planting, a lawn, trees, water, a strong structure, interest through the year. Each must have a selection of these and some of the owners will have their personal specialized interest: topiary, sculpture, scent, roses, spring bulbs and autumn colour, perennial or mixed borders and vegetables.

Historic gardens must be included. Helmingham Hall in Suffolk dates back to 1485, the property owned continuously since then by the Tollemache family; the garden, cultivated for several generations, has been brought to its present perfection by Xa and Tim Tollemache. Benington Lordship in Hertfordshire, owned by the Bott family since 1910, was a Saxon stronghold and medieval ruins are incorporated into the garden; today it has the atmosphere of a property surrounded by indigenous trees. It has year-long interest with autumn and winter colour, the February spectacle of its snowdrop-filled moat and herbaceous borders through summer and autumn.

Gardens made early this century before the First World War, and those in the 1920s and 1930s, include Kiftsgate Court in Gloucestershire, owned and maintained by the same family for three generations. Now Anne and her husband John Chambers are in charge.

Great Dixter, eighty years ago the combined work of Nathaniel Lloyd and Sir Edwin Lutyens, is now cared for by the great gardener and plantsman Christopher Lloyd. I had to include a garden designed by both Gertrude Jekyll and Lutyens, and Folly Farm, near Reading, was chosen. The design, the walls, the great yew hedges and the brick and stone paths are still as Lutyens designed them in 1912 and the planting today is much as Jekyll planned.

Three of my chosen gardens, created in recent years, are completely different in character. Chilcombe House in Dorset, with new planting inside old stone walls, is the artist's garden, and relies on structure and carefully chosen colour combinations and foliage effects. David Hicks' garden at The Grove in Oxfordshire is the best recent example in England of an architectural garden, designed as an extension of his house. Each window has its view into 'rooms' with walls of clipped hedges and pleached trees. Winfield House in Regents Park, London, is not in the country and is the home of the American Ambassador, but I wanted to include it for in essence it is both country and English. Walking here you could well be in the heart of the countryside and it has the atmosphere of an English garden.

Six of my twelve gardens have united husband and wife teams and two that are outstanding for this are the Manor House at Bledlow and Holker

Hall in Cumbria. Bledlow, the home of Peter and Iona Carrington, and one of my favourite gardens, has matured as their joint hobby, a relaxation from a busy public life. Now, through their expertise, it has matured with Iona's knowledge of plants and Peter's original and creative talent. It is essentially a family home and so is Holker Hall, another of my favourite gardens. Grania and Hugh Cavendish have found the solution of having the garden open to the public and keeping their own garden around the house quite private. Grania has an expert eye for structure and for plants so everything is in harmony and the garden feels really loved. Hugh's knowledge of all the trees and shrubs in the woodland is comprehensive; inspired by his grandmother when he was young, he has grown up with them and is always adding to the collection.

I wanted to include one garden I had helped to design, so selected Elton John's. It is never open to the public, but a glimpse in this book and on television is a chance to enjoy his taste – the first thought he passed on to me was his love of cottage garden flowers; now his horizon has widened, and his garden is changing.

Making the television series which *The English Country Garden* accompanies took me through the gardening year, and for this reason the book is divided into spring, summer, autumn and winter. Within these chapters I describe features that are at their best during a particular season – but within the context of a garden as a whole. Gardening is a total concept and to be successful should achieve year-long interest, from the emergence of spring bulbs to the colour of mixed borders in summer, the red-gold glory of foliage in autumn and the architectural outlines of trees and shrubs in winter. It is a continuous process, and one of the most rewarding aspects of my visits was the many opportunities they gave me to exchange theories about gardening with like-minded enthusiasts who, whether their gardens are their relaxation or their livelihood, are the inheritors of a long and very English tradition. Inevitably, these discussions turned my thoughts back to my own Barnsley House, which is also featured in this book. All this is reflected in these chapters.

England is a land of beautiful gardens and I am grateful to have had this opportunity to describe twelve of them for *The English Country Garden*.

ROSEMARY VEREY

S P R I N G

*A*s spring arrives the earth warms up and you can feel, as well as see, the plants growing daily. Narcissus and daffodils create a crescendo of colour, gold and cream to complement the purple honesty and blue grape hyacinths. Ornamental cherries and crab apples bring clouds of crimson, pink and white while the leaves on our trees and shrubs have a wonderful freshness as they unfurl. Magnolias open their glistening white cups and candle-shaped flower clusters stand erect on the chestnuts. It is all there for us to see.

There is the characteristic scent of grass clippings as mowing our lawns becomes a weekly event, so the mower must be kept in good order.

In the vegetable garden sprouting broccoli, freshly picked, is delicious, lettuces are hearting up and the herbs to go with them have their best flavour.

From mid-April until mid-June a well-established asparagus bed gives a twice-weekly picking.

Remember the viburnums and lilacs for their scent.

*G*reat Dixter in spring. It would have been a great privilege to have met and talked with Christopher Lloyd's mother for it was she, earlier this century who, inspired by Botticelli's 'Primavera', raised from seed and planted the flowers in the grassland at Dixter. Christo, with his understanding of plants, has encouraged these narcissus, fritillaries and wood anemones to grow through the grass. This is not mown until August, when the seeds have ripened and fallen, to allow these beauties to multiply over the years.

GREAT DIXTER

*T*he secret of Great Dixter's charm is the way in which the garden enfolds the manor house on all sides with trees, hedges and topiary, everywhere richly planted. It is as though the garden's role is to protect the ancient farmhouse. Only a century ago it stood isolated in pasture land, which supported both the farmer and his cattle. Now it is the great gardener Christopher Lloyd who protects the house and maintains the beauty of the garden. This half-timbered manor house is part fifteenth century, with part added early in this century to incorporate a derelict sixteenth-century yeoman's house moved from nearby Benenden.

In 1910 the property, having stood empty for ten years, was bought by Nathaniel Lloyd and his wife, and with Sir Edwin Lutyens as their architect they restored and enlarged the house. By June 1912 they were able to move in. It became their family home, where six children were reared. Indoors there was a staff of five; outdoors in those early years, as the garden grew, there were nine gardeners.

Christopher Lloyd, who lives here now amid a constant flow of visitors, was born in the house in 1921, and when you meet him or watch him working in the garden, you instinctively realize that he is truly part of the place. He understands, enjoys and has watched over Great Dixter for so many years, knowing every plant, every idiosyncrasy of the roof, the chimneys and the Great Hall, every detail of the garden plan drawn up for his father by Sir Edwin Lutyens. As a child he looked through the 'crawling window', built especially by Lutyens for anyone less than three feet tall to peep through and enjoy views of the garden below.

The old farm buildings were not pulled down to make way for new garden follies, but instead cleverly incorporated into Lutyens' plan, as were the old cattle yards. The three oast houses became a feature of the west side, their white cowls turning in the wind. Next to them, an old barn with a magnificent long red-tiled roof reaching nearly to the ground protects plants and helps to create a favourable microclimate. For this barn garden,

*T*he host of golden daffodils flowering in the orchard on the south side of the house appears every spring, revealing for how great a number of years this garden has been tended. Every plant in our gardens needs our care, but the daffodils, so thickly massed together, are never fed, otherwise the turf ingredients become coarse and the weaker plants are squeezed out. Their leaves are allowed to die down naturally. ❧

Lutyens' plan shows a central lawn; now there is a more interesting sunk garden with an octagonal pool, designed by Nathaniel Lloyd in the early 1920s. He (like his son Christopher) had an unerring eye for architectural proportion, so it is not surprising that the barn garden is satisfying at all times of the year, with its strong structure and, in recent years, Christo's planting.

Nathaniel was very keen on the art of topiary, and it was he who dreamed up the idea of making bird topiary in the high garden, each character sitting atop a pyramidal yew plinth. Originally they were a 'menagerie', referred to by Mrs Lloyd as 'a Parliament of birds'; now they are all mature peacocks! Ten are still gathered around a central paved area, and the other eight face each other in pairs on the radiating paths. Clipping starts from September on, and the sharp outlines of the yews remain until early summer encourages new growth. On the topiary lawn on the south-west side of the house, some specimens are representational, like the pair of coffee pots; others have developed into geometrical shapes – as their growth and the clippers decreed.

Nathaniel was also keen on planting yew hedges wherever a division or windbreak was needed, overruling Lutyens' wish to build more walls. Lutyens had a tremendous flair for combining brick, stone and slate in his designs, giving a warmth and an originality which set off the walls, paths

*T*he approach from the front gate along the straight flagstone path takes you directly to the front porch. On each side carefully selected bulbs have been naturalizing since Christo's mother became enchanted by Botticelli's 'Primavera'.

Before the important trees here – *Crataegus prunifolia* and *C. laciniata* – come into leaf, there are snowdrops followed by *Crocus chrysanthus* and *C. tommasinianus*. Then the Lent daffodils, *Narcissus pseudonarcissus*, snakeshead fritillaries and North American camassias.

As well as the bulbs, enjoy the strong horizontal lines of the house, the Tudor-style chimneys added by Lutyens, and the fifteenth-century porch. But you must walk beyond the yew hedges before the full beauty of the house is revealed.

and steps and inviting you to take notes and photographs to remind you of ideas for your own garden.

Springtime is an awakening. Reynolds Hole, Dean of Rochester, writing at the start of the twentieth century, recommended that to have a garden full you should keep on propagating. My dictum is that every autumn the gardener must order new bulbs to add to the borders and to every possible corner. Each year some bulbs will multiply, while others will fall victim to mice, squirrels or a virus. In an old-established garden such as Great Dixter, there has inevitably been a continuous build-up of bulbs.

Christo's mother admired the Swiss Alpine meadows in springtime, and since 1912 several areas, principally close to the house, have been treated as meadows; Christo has perfected the art of meadow-management better than anyone else I know in England.

Enter the front gate and the straight flagstone path takes you directly towards the porch. Christo will point out – if you have not already noticed – that the porch has a lean on it which must have happened at an early age. Here, from spring to autumn, there are always plants arrayed in abundance – in clay pots which, being heavy, are less likely to be blown over. (Another hint, often neglected, is to give a liquid feed once a week when the plants are growing strongly.) Here in early spring you will find small pots of miniature Narcissus 'Tête-à-Tête' and *Anemone blanda* 'White Splendour', which can do a year's service here before joining others in the meadow garden. Slugs, as I've discovered, can play havoc with some of the more costly bulbs (as well as with hostas) – while half a dozen can be safe and look exciting in a pot, a dozen may well be slug-ravaged in the border. Fritillaries come to mind – *Fritillaria pallidiflora* and *F. persica,* especially *F. p.* 'Adiyaman'. You can find such beauties displayed every spring at Royal Horticultural Society shows in Vincent Square. Even the large-garden owner who loves great displays must long for small intimate moments of beauty – pots can be the answer.

In my own borders I constantly wonder what will provide colour next week, but a display of pots is movable, and with plenty of planning there will always be a flowering substitute to take over. It may be hyacinths, tulips, or annuals like cornflowers or corn marigolds from an autumn sowing. Then in summer and autumn lilies will become the most important characters.

On each side of the flagstone entrance path, carefully selected bulbs have naturalized under and around an old pear tree and two hawthorns, *Crataegus tanacetifolia* and *C. laciniata*; both of these have grey-green, rather downy leaves.

The snowdrops start to push through in January, ready for their two months' display, together with *Crocus chrysanthus* and *C. tommasinianus.* Real gardeners love plants which will self-seed, and these crocus, if they

appreciate your garden soil, will eventually create a pale mauve carpet. There are drifts of Lent daffodils, *Narcissus pseudonarcissus,* originally grown from seed by Mrs Lloyd and now established to flower after the crocus.

However much this northern forecourt holds your attention you must move on, through the wall garden, to discover the other meadow areas, the upper moat and the orchard. In the former you will find lots of polyanthus, and snakeshead fritillaries – again raised from seed – *Anemone apennina, Iris latifolia* and *Leucojum aestivum.* It is all a lesson in how well our native plants will do in meadow grass, and combine with others such as the Dutch crocus and cyclamen. But the right treatment, and patience, are essential. Christo's sound advice is that most grassland plants thrive best on poor soil. There are two flowering seasons, January to July and then August to October. The grass is mown as low as possible twice a year – at the end of July and in late autumn (sometimes in early December).

ABOVE *W*e can learn from Christopher Lloyd the importance of mass planting of bulbs to bring the garden alive in spring. An April scene, looking through the *Tulipa* 'Red Matador' growing in the long border, over the stone path to a view across the orchard.

The daffodils are planted in alternate areas of yellow and white varieties, but with sufficient space between them to allow room for crocuses, snowdrops and native orchids.

A lesson I learnt from the late Countess Münster's garden at Bampton is the importance of planting narcissus in drifts of the same variety, so colours are not mixed. If spaces are left between them for other features to come on later, these will direct your attention from the dying daffodil leaves. Christo in his meadow has early purple orchids, *Orchis mascula*, and the spotted orchid, *Dactylorhiza fuchsii*. Both of these will self-sow if the seeds fall in an undisturbed place.

In May the dominant flower in the entrance meadow is *Camassia quamash*, a 60 cm (2 ft) tall blue flowered bulb native to the north-west of America. Christopher first planted these many years ago when they were comparatively cheap and easy to get – now Prince Charles has them in his meadow garden where they flower at the same time as the dark purple tulip 'The Bishop'. Christo's have increased – I hope those at Highgrove will do the same.

Christo says that tulips are his favourite spring bulbs. They appreciate his heavy soil and will flower in the same place for as long as twenty-five years. I wish ours would at Barnsley, but perhaps we do not plant them deeply enough. Some tulips he treats as bedding plants, lifting them after flowering to make way for summer bedding.

Most of the borders at Dixter are a mixture of shrubs and perennials, with highlights of annuals, but in the solar garden beside the front porch, while there is always colour, the planting has a more formal plan. The L-shaped bed has a brick wall behind it, and a permanent background planting of white Japanese anemones, which flower from August through to October and will enhance any of Christo's colour schemes. The front half of the bed is devoted to annuals and bedding plants, which Christo changes at least twice a year, sometimes three times; the colour scheme is different each year. Wallflowers and tulips may start the display, and will be dug up as soon as they show signs of fading. If the bedding (planted the previous autumn) is of sweet Williams or border carnations (from seed), the first changeover will not come until mid-July. Following on might be dahlias from seed or nasturtiums (from pots) or marigolds, which earlier in the season were lined out in readiness in the open ground. Every year it is something different, experiment being the spice of life to Christo and his gardener Fergus Garrett.

Garden visitors love to associate

RIGHT *P*lants in pots, massed in front of the porch, are a handsome feature at Great Dixter. Christo and his head gardener, Fergus Garrett, nurture these in the necessary greenhouse and standing-ground area until they come into flower.

On this April day purple *Tulipa* 'Greuze' and an unknown yellow tulip stand beside the white azalea and the interesting *Gladiolus* × *colvillei*. In the foreground the leaves of *Beschorneria yuccoides* play their green and spiky part.

parts of a large garden with their own smaller ones – so do I. If I could choose one part of Great Dixter's garden to reproduce at Barnsley, it would be the sunk garden – remembering that I could not have the same weathered red-brick background on two sides: our walls and roofs in the Cotswolds are oolitic limestone, full of fossils but with a mellow, honey-coloured texture.

When a garden is totally satisfying, I sometimes try to analyse why – what are the individual features which make up the whole picture? Here in the sunk garden it is changes of level. You step down to the pond, but this is not square: it is octagonal, with two long sides. Some of the paths are grass and some stone, giving a difference of texture. The light varies according to the time of day. The long barn with its steeply slanting red roof faces east and gets the sun for most of the day, and has a vigorous climbing white solanum, while three dramatically pruned old figs have taken over the wall of the south-facing smaller barn.

Wander here in spring to find lovely hummocks of *Eupatoria polychroma*, with tulips and developing hosta leaves. There are spring-flowering shrubs – white *Exochorda × macrantha* 'The Bride' with yellow jonquils around it, and golden *Coronilla valentina* with blue *Scilla siberica* (Christo hopes their flowering will coincide). In April and May *Prunus tenella* is interplanted with *Arabis caucasica* 'Flore Pleno'.

By May the long border holds increasing interest. Young leaves of *Euonymus × fortunei* 'Silver Queen' are fresh with their pale yellow margins, and magenta flower spikes of *Gladiolus bysantinus* push through its low branches. Peonies, the rich crimson doubles, look wonderful near the bush willow, *Salix helvetica,* and London Pride in the high garden.

If I were told I could only spend one more day of my life in any garden other than my own, being taken round by the owner, I would drive to Great Dixter to see Christopher Lloyd, no matter what time of year. Here is a perfect entity – Sir Edwin Lutyens' masterly garden plan fits the house perfectly, Nathaniel Lloyd's architectural understanding is apparent, but Christopher Lloyd's genius as a gardener and plant lover radiates through-out the garden today. He loves and knows his plants, has an innate sense of design, an insatiable desire to experiment, and a sense of humour – in his garden and his friendships.

*T*he barn garden has a fascination all through the year. In spring it is its freshness which appeals, with the white *Exochorda × macrantha* 'The Bride', hummocks of *Euphorbia polychroma*, yellow jonquils, and the golden *Coronilla valentina* with *Scilla siberica* nearby. There are splashes of red created by the tulips and polyanthus. Notice how Edwin Lutyens treated the coping on the top of the wall. The York stone paving is convenient to walk on, though slippery on wet days. The white-flowered shrub in the centre of the picture is *Prunus glandulosa* 'Alba Plena'.

The solar room overlooks this garden and is a focal point from it.

HELMINGHAM HALL

*E*nthusiasm is infectious, and that which Lady Tollemache feels for her garden and for growing plants must inspire many of the visitors who come to Helmingham. She has certainly fired me with new ideas.

The Tollemache family have lived at Helmingham Hall for 500 years, some generations caring for its well-being more than others. The present house was built in 1490 on the site of an older house and Lord and Lady Tollemache – Tim and Xa – inherited the property and took up residence here in 1975.

Tim farms and manages the estate, and with her great energy, imagination and taste, Xa has brought new life to the garden. On the east side of the house she has created knot gardens and a new rose garden, and on the west side she has simplified the planting of the parterre, eliminating time-consuming bedding-out. The walled kitchen garden has seen a revival under the care of the head gardener, Mr Roy Balaam.

The gardens at Helmingham do not open officially until the end of April, but if you are fortunate enough to walk through the grounds earlier in the month you will find primroses, daffodils and early narcissus naturalized on the east side along the bank containing the moat and overlooking the knot and herb gardens. The knot gardens look freshest in spring when bulbs are flowering, the herbs are low, and you can see the designs most clearly.

Everything in the knot gardens has its meaning or symbolism. There are eight beds, each 3 metres (10 ft 6 in) square, four either side of a central grass path 3.5 metres (11 ft 6 in) wide which runs through this whole garden, including the rose beds. On your left as you look down from the bank are four beds with elaborate knot designs, and on your right are four divided into triangles for herb-growing.

I first visited Helmingham about fifteen years ago, and remember being impressed with the proposed patterns for these knots, which Xa and Tim were thinking up. They were very much influenced and helped by Lady Salisbury, who is THE twentieth-century expert on Elizabethan gardens, especially knots. When designing knots, it is appropriate to choose motifs which are characteristic of the house, or the owners. In this case Lord and Lady Tollemache's initials – 'A' for Alexandra and 'T' for Timothy – have been used. Enclosed in two squares, the 'threads' drawing their initials are of box, some darker, some lighter in colour.

The other motif used is the important Tollemache fret, which appears throughout the house and garden: on the shield of their coat of arms, in the brickwork of the house, and on the balustrade of the drawbridge. In the knot garden, diagonally between the initialled squares, two more display this fret pattern. All four squares are full of flowers introduced to England before 1750. Spring flowers include grape hyacinths, alliums (which were called moly), pulsatilla, anemones, winter aconites (winter wolfesbane), hepatica, violas, nigella, *Helleborus niger*. In summer there are caltha, malva,

*H*elmingham Hall, built in 1490, is surrounded by a deep moat. The walled garden on the west side of the house has another, narrower moat around it, where these daffodils grow on its bank. They bloom before the blossoms on the apple and pear trees open. The mown grass around the trees adds a contrasting texture, especially in spring when the slope of the bank is emphasized by the mass of golden daffodils. Beyond the railings on the right lies the ancient parkland. ❧

hollyhocks, toadflax, feverfew, marigolds, 'gilloflowers', peonies, soapwort, campanulas and others. Box edging, kept low, divides each of the four herb beds into six triangles, and these are generously filled with medicinal and cooking herbs grown in Tudor times.

On the west side of the house, a grass path with classical stone figures at each end runs along the side of the moat, and on the bank of the moat more primroses and narcissus start blooming in March. Here Dinah, Lady Tollemache, Xa's mother-in-law, planted a border of Hybrid Musk roses under the west wall of the potager, and a parterre garden for interest on the lawn. This was in 1965, and many of her roses survive today.

WOODSIDE

*T*he decision as to whether or not you can say 'yes' to a prospective client is often difficult. When Elton John's personal assistant, Robert Key, rang me and mentioned the name 'Woodside', my thoughts immediately turned to the mid eighteenth-century artist Thomas Robins, who specialized in painting English rococo gardens. Sure enough, there in John Harris' book *Gardens of Delight* (published in 1978) were watercolours showing Woodside garden in the 1750s. In America I found a copy of the limited edition, which I bought for Elton.

I told Robert Key that I would like to be involved, without – at that moment – being aware of the size of the project. I made my first visit in October 1987, then heard nothing until February 1988, just as I was leaving for the United States. When I was asked for a detailed overall plan 'almost at once', I explained that gardening is a long-term project – shrubs and trees need time to grow to maturity.

However, to work for Elton John in an eighteenth-century rococo garden was an irresistible enticement. I could not keep to their immediate deadline, so I asked Gordon Taylor and Guy Cooper (freelance designers) if they would become involved. They agreed and for four years one or both of them went daily to Woodside to oversee the work. Together we planned the general layout with borders, avenues, a lake and areas of differing characters.

One of my first designs was the white garden. The French windows of the drawing room open on to a stone-paved terrace, and Elton told me that this was where he would entertain his friends on summer evenings. A white garden would provide the perfect setting for spring and summer parties. It was to be a peaceful place, a restful interlude among the variety of themes incorporated in the whole garden. There were various factors to be considered: Elton would look down on this from his bedroom and walk into it from his drawing room. There was an existing oak tree and a boundary thuya hedge, both of which at this stage he was keen to keep.

I love symmetry, and believe that for a garden beside the house where you entertain, the borders should be curving, without awkward, acute corners.

Spring is easy, using white narcissus and daffodils. Originally in 1991 we planted *Narcissus* 'Mount Hood' and *N.* 'White Lion', as well as a few white hyacinths, and we were able to add many of these among and around the white-flowered lamium. Each year different white bulbs may be added. In 1995 Helen Finch, then head gardener, had a group of *N.* 'Rippling Water' looking good with white pulmonaria, and the white winter pansies were doing well. In late spring the elegant lily-flowered *Tulipa* 'White Triumphator' hold the stage, echoing the stems of *Populus alba* 'Richardii' and the flowers of *Spiraea* 'Arguta'.

Through the season there is a plethora of white flowers to choose from,

*Y*ou can walk into the scented garden from the dining room on the south side. I planned it to give a fragrance at all times of the year. The design must be interesting as it is overlooked from several windows. The paths are narrow and winding, so visitors – and Elton – will stroll single-file along them, enjoying the fragrance of roses, heliotrope, honeysuckles and philadelphus in summer, and the bulbs and sarcococca in springtime.

The winding brick paths are lined with clipped box and sage and the straight paths with lavender. For height – an important dimension – there are standard bays and viburnums. Pots with seasonal scented plants are kept around the pavilion.

The French windows of the drawing room open on to a stone-paved terrace where Elton likes to entertain his friends on summer evenings. I love symmetry and then to infill with an exuberance of plants, and this white garden provided the perfect setting for spring and summer parties.

The colour scheme in these four curving borders is kept to white, grey, green and some yellow – white narcissus and tulips, penstemon and parahebe, spiraea and hydrangeas. Sadly (for me), Elton decided he wanted an Italian garden, so after six years my white garden has gone, statues and vistas have taken over. I wonder, does an Italian garden blend with and complement an English Regency house? This picture was taken before Charlie 'scalloped' the thuya hedge.

and yet it is fun when another colour creeps in. I was amused – and hope Elton was too – with the yellow wallflowers. In summer 1994 Helen grew the wallflower 'White Wonder' from seed. She commented, 'It said on the seed packet it was white, so we planted them out with great expectations, and when they bloomed they were pale yellow.' Personally I thought they looked extremely good with the grey-leaved white stocks, providing an innuendo of white to palest yellow.

The first year we had black tulips. This was an idea I had copied from a photograph in Russell Page's book *The Education of a Gardener,* putting black and white tulips between grey-foliage plants.

Frost in the English garden is capricious, and one night in April it can hit the emerging leaves of the herbaceous plants. On my visit the cimicifuga and the white dicentra were lying low, but I had confidence they would recover. The annual white larkspurs planted out in early April to give them a good start had a setback too – but they would come on and flower in July and August, instead of June as planned.

In these white borders, as well as annuals and shrubs, there is a mixture of hardy perennials. The stand-bys are white dame's violets (*Hesperis matronalis),* goat's rue (*Galega officinalis), Astrantia major, Anaphalis triplinervis* and *Phlox paniculata* 'White Admiral'. Some of these are just off-white, which makes the true whites glisten even whiter.

Helen and I took special care of the edging plants. *Campanula persicifolia alba* is at the front so it can be constantly dead-headed to encourage it to go on flowering. *Viola cornuta* Alba Group threads its way through the dictamnus and white potentilla. There are dianthus and *Campanula carpatica* with white rock roses and santolina.

I decided that the edge of the paved terrace should have a very simple planting – rosemary one end and santolina the other, with alternating white parahebe and the grey-leaved *Hebe topiaria.* This worked well for two years, but the designer and the gardener must always realize that plants develop, grow old, and may need replacing with young specimens. When I make planting plans for borders I like to rough them out on paper, then spend time on site placing each plant myself, giving it its correct spacing and seeing how the drifts will work together and where there is room to drop in another plant – maybe contrasting in outline or leaf shape. This is the final touch which helps to make a border.

Before leaving the design of the white garden I had more thoughts! The horizontal top of the thuya hedge was uninteresting – why do hedges have to have flat tops? – so I suggested to Charlie, who was then doing all the clipping, that he should scallop it. My inspiration came from Harry Ladew's garden in Maryland, USA, where the hedges not only have 'swags' but also 'windows'.

So Charlie, with an eye for precision, clipped the hedge horizontally for one metre (3 ft), and then shaped the swags with a rope tied to two sticks inserted into the hedge.

A white garden is essentially peaceful – or should be – but you can learn here that rules are often made to be broken, so do not hold too fast to the word 'white'. Vita Sackville-West thought up the idea of a white garden during a snowstorm – presumably in wintertime when the garden was asleep, so a blue flower with a white streak or a white flower with a gold splash could well fit into the plan as she imagined seeing it between the snowflakes. I believe pansies in spring, salvias and mallows in summer, and lobelia in autumn can all take part in this garden as long as there is a major element of white.

When Elton came back unexpectedly, it was satisfactory to be able to provide him with a show. On stage he holds the audience: why should his borders not do the same for him? Like all creative people, his imagination moves on, and now the white garden has been replaced by an Italian garden designed by Sir Roy Strong.

In winter 1992, when the basic groundwork on the gardens immediately round the house had been completed, Helen (then head gardener) and I decided it was time to work on the 7.6 hectare (19 acre) woodland, so that Elton could enjoy walking here – in springtime, especially, when the narcissus and bluebells are at their best.

The woodland offered great scope, and I turned again to the eighteenth-century paintings of Thomas Robins. He shows an exciting Chinese kiosk in a formal setting hidden in the wood, where gardeners are scything, raking, rolling and sweeping in a romantic style. On one side of the kiosk sheep and cattle graze in a meadow framed by wide, straight, raised paths with a conveniently placed seat and behind maturing trees. On the other side winding paths lead through more woodland – a style and atmosphere we have tried to emulate 240 years later. It is sad that there are no contemporary accounts to turn to for more advice. A summer-house in the distance looks down on the scene from a gently rolling hillside fringed with trees, which I take to be Crimp Hill. The lack of precise evidence makes me aware of the importance of documentation, so that future generations can copy and comprehend when work is carried out on historic gardens.

When working in the woodland we discovered a few 'hard standings', where follies could well once have been sited – but more of this later.

Our first task was to cut back many of the evergreens, especially the Portugal laurels – once, no doubt, planned to be kept well shaped but now spilling out and over the original paths. Their character had changed from clipped evergreen bushes to sprawling shrubs. Many of the fine deciduous trees were also in serious need of surgery.

We realized that no new planting could be done until the rabbit and deer population was controlled. The rabbits could not be got rid of until their

Old clay oil-jars flank the main gate into the potager. All eight gateways and the surrounding fence have now been painted a rich mulberry colour. A 1.8 metre (6 ft) grass path forms the main axis leading to the central pool where four white marble fish spout water. The four quadrants are divided by a mixture of grass and brick paths, creating patterns of narrow beds.

Some beds are used for growing flowers for picking for the house, and others for permanent planting such as rhubarb, artichokes and strawberries. In the other beds a strict rotation of crops is kept to give the best results.

homes among the overgrown brambles were bulldozed. Russell Warner, who had done much of the landscaping work in the garden, came in with his machines and chainsaw. Where he cleared the worst entanglement of brambles, we have made an open area with a winding diagonal mown path running through. Among the newly planted trees here are *Acer griseum, Ptelea trifoliata, Styrax japonica, Halesia manticola*, underplanted with narcissus and 500 wild flowers grown in plugs. To prevent the brambles regrowing Helen inaugurated a carefully arranged three-times-a-year mowing programme.

We marked trees which needed careful attention and those whose branches encroached on the pathways. Soon the whole scene was changed. Then Elton agreed to have a deer fence erected around the major part of the property. This was wonderful for the woodland, and even better for the gardens around the house, where the deer and rabbits between them devoured much of the young growth.

Guy Cooper and Gordon Taylor achieved two important successes in the woodland. They had the clay-lined pool cleared of debris and years of fallen leaves, and the banks were stabilized. The pond has remained dark and clear ever since. Helen has an interesting theory that the water in a woodland pool keeps itself clear; the latest research suggests that leaves falling into the water create a chemical reaction, releasing an algae inhibitor, in the same way as barley straw. It certainly works here, but I wonder how often the decayed leaves should be taken out. Surprisingly, there is no blanket weed either – a pest in many pools – because of the overhanging trees.

With the clear dark water, there are wonderful reflections of the surrounding trees and of the underplanting we have done more recently. The gentle ripple on the water's surface gives an extra interest and a reflected vibration to the sword-like leaves of the variegated acorus (planted in May 1993). As the pool is clay-lined, the surrounding edges are not damp, but we have used a mixture of shade-loving plants and those in harmony with a water setting. In spring there are candelabra primulas, *Euphorbia robbiae, Helleborus foetidus* and *H. argutifolius,* and lots of ferns. The lysichiton are doing well, and so are *Phlomis russeliana* and the marsh marigolds.

Seeing this pool in spring, I was full of hope that Elton finds time to walk here when he is at home. Now there is a perfect way into the woodland, over the wooden bridge framed by two old oak trees, and soon you come to this pool. You can walk all round it, as we did. As we wandered on, Helen said, 'Well, you never know what you're going to find in a wood like this', we rounded a corner – and there was a fibreglass dinosaur, 'Daisy', looking as though she was about to spring out of the undergrowth.

When Daisy first arrived at Woodside, as a present from George

Harrison, she was isolated on the lawn with no planting around her. My reaction was that she must find her way into the woodland – a more appropriate setting for her. She moved in by helicopter, cleverly arranged by Guy and Gordon. It must have been a bit of a shock for her, and now she duly responds by surprising unknowing visitors, especially after dark when an infra-red sensor is automatically set to light her up. Helen and her gardeners did good work with the planting around her. There are *Trachycarpus fortunei,* variegated phormium and *Nandina domestica* amongst the laurels. It is important to keep the mystery with enough appropriate shrubs close by, but her full size must be visible, from her tail to her large back legs and her glittering eye.

A major operation when all the cutting down and clearing had been completed was to put a 7.5 cm (3 in) layer of wood chippings on to all the main paths. There was much work involved, but now it gives a lovely, natural, springing surface – a joy to walk on.

More surprises are to come, after strolling through clearings where old beech and oak trees have been freed of the tangle of the undergrowth so their boles stand out like pillars in a cloister – a perfect place for bluebells

*I*n one corner of the woodland a pool once filled with debris and fallen leaves has been cleaned out and clay-lined. The dark water has wonderful reflections of the surrounding oak and holly trees and has remained crystal-clear without algae or blanket weed. It is suggested that leaves falling into the water create a chemical reaction, releasing an algae inhibitor, in the same way as barley straw.

Fallen leaves are allowed to remain on the woodland floor, providing humus where a mix of native and introduced plants flourish and candelabra primulas, primroses and euphorbias contrast with the sword-like leaves of variegated iris and sedges. Each year the planting improves, greatly helped by the deer-proof fencing which contains this area of the wood.

and wild orchids. From here you can choose your route according to your whim or the weather – this is the joy of the woodland.

Helen guided me to the right, determined that I should appreciate Elton's sense of humour and amusement with late twentieth-century collectables. Who else would you expect to hide a red telephone kiosk and pillar box (ERII) in the middle of an eighteenth-century wood? Both are sited on brick standings, where a statue or folly once stood in the rococo setting. Now a British Telecom telephone box has arrived – though not connected to the outside world. The modern trend is to turn these into sophisticated showers to be used to clean off after a salt water or chlorinated swim. True to form, there inside is a sylph-like lady – Aphrodite, I was certain – making a call. It must have been to Elton – there is a connection from the woodland to the house. Not far away in the same glade is a round red pillar box. If the telephone does not work, maybe the postman will collect the Christmas post on time.

When you step outside the fence where the deer still roam you can immediately see the difference, but luckily they do not eat and spoil the amazing dog rose walk in the sunny glade. Though not pruned for years, this still performs with scented flowers and a mass of coloured hips. Now pathways are mown through so everyone can enjoy them, and Helen has planted thousands of bluebells in the shady glade.

This walk brings you back to the pond and the wooden bridge. With more time you can discover other parts of the woodland, using the network of wood-chip paths.

*D*aisy the dinosaur dominates her corner of the woodland garden. Though friendly, when her eyes light up she gives you an initial surprise – or is it shock? – as she appears ready to leap out and catch you on your evening stroll. After cutting back overgrown Portugal laurels, an ideal spot was found for her. She was given to Elton as a present from George Harrison and has found her final resting place surrounded by suitably prehistoric-looking *Trachycarpus fortunei*, phormiums and nandina amongst the evergreen laurels.

FOLLY FARM

*F*olly Farm was up for sale, and on a cold wet day in February 1951 Mr and Mrs Hugh Astor, newly married, went to see the property. They came back again in April, when the sun was shining and the many spring bulbs and flowering cherries were at their best. They fell in love with the place and, in spite of its wartime neglect, decided to buy it. Since then it has become a much-loved family home.

They knew that the original farmhouse had been enlarged by Sir Edwin Lutyens in 1906, and that Gertrude Jekyll had designed the garden, but it was not until they had been there for several years that they fully understood the importance of the design, and the relationship between house and garden. From the windows on the south side there are vistas along the canal and the flower parterre, and views into the tank cloister. Twenty years later,

Hugh Astor acquired the garden plans, showing how Gertrude Jekyll's planting complemented and softened the strong architectural lines imposed by Lutyens. We will never know which of these two great designers had the final say.

In July 1916 Mrs Merton, widow of the owner, lent Folly Farm to the Lutyens family. By all accounts this was the only occasion in which he had the opportunity to live in one of the houses he had designed. He and his family were so happy there, dead-heading roses, fishing for goldfish and studying his design patterns. Through Mrs Merton's eyes we can begin to understand the intricacies of his mind and his attention to detail, which portrays itself in all his houses.

On my visit in April Mr Honour, the present head gardener, who has

*A*t the end of the lime walk designed by Gertrude Jekyll, the white *Narcissus* 'Thalia' have their April display after the snowdrops and aconites have played their part. On the left the stone figure of 'François' presides over Emi-Lu's white garden, where once a hornbeam arbour surrounded a deep 'bath' of dark water. Now the discipline of the planting of foxgloves, lilies, 'Iceberg' roses and white-flowered hebes is refreshing after the exuberance of the flower parterre and the rose garden. Every garden should have a quiet corner where we may meditate and refresh our spirit.

*S*pring is an especially joyous time in the garden at Folly Farm. This photograph, taken across the meadow looking towards the south and west sides of the house, has hosts of naturalized 'King Alfred' and 'Golden Harvest' daffodils – probably part of Gertrude Jekyll's original planting plan of 1912. Beyond them, the yew hedge emphatically divides the formal garden from this outer sanctuary.

From here is a perfect view of the complex design of roofs and chimneys, always important features in Lutyens' houses. Gardens must always be moving forward, and Mr Honour, who has worked here for thirty-five years, has planted these *Sorbus* 'Joseph Rock', *Malus* 'Golden Hornet', *Prunus* 'Hokosai' and *P. subhirtella* 'Rubra Pendula' trees for their spring blossom and autumn colour. I would love Gertrude Jekyll and Sir Edwin Lutyens to see this scene today as they planned it eighty years ago.

worked here for thirty-five years, showed me the cherry trees, apples, pears and greengages that grow and flower in the 'rough grass area' planted with many daffodils – 'King Alfred', 'Ice King', 'Sir Winston Churchill', 'Golden Harvest'. Then there are the old varieties, unnamed, which may have been growing there since before the First World War. All these daffodils, including the distinctive pheasant-eye narcissi, are naturalized.

Tulips do not survive in grass as daffodils will, so each autumn Mr Honour orders 500 red 'Apeldoorn' tulips to plant among the daffodils, and as you can imagine these give a vibrant splash of colour later in the season – red through green.

In the sunken rose garden two lily-flowered tulips have been chosen: 'China Pink' are planted between the roses, and 'White Triumphator'

amongst the lavender in the central feature of this garden. The 'White Triumphator' are also used beside the barn at the front of the house, and between hostas in the white garden, where earlier the low-growing *greigii* tulips 'Red Riding Hood', with unusual striped leaves, grow among the bluebells.

Mr Honour always shows the bulb list to Mrs Astor for her approval. Every year he orders white crocus, as I do for Barnsley House garden; at Folly Farm they grow under the lime and oak trees. Hellebores are not

Seen from one side, the tank cloister fits neatly between two wings of the house – an extension Lutyens made in 1912 for Zachary Merton. The dark water in the tank reflects the strong buttresses appearing to support the dramatic roof with its small dormer windows.

Emi-Lu and Hugh like to sit here when it is warm enough, and on wet days they can enjoy the rain falling on the water. Lutyens often put steps by water, and the pattern is typically geometric. The treads are smooth stone, just overhanging the risers made with red slate and mortar. The strong horizontal lines are softened by aubrieta which has found its way through cracks.

No book about English country gardens would be complete without a Gertrude Jekyll garden incorporating Lutyens' distinctive stone and brickwork. Laid several decades ago, these unusually shaped bricks (23 × 5 cm/9 × 2 in) have had enough years to mellow and grow moss and lichen. When making paths in your garden, turn to Lutyens' patterns for inspiration.

Walking around the garden, we must always remember to look up as well as down, not to miss the climbers and trees overhead. At Folly Farm you must always do both so you will be inspired by ideas for patterns of paving, steps and archways.

forgotten and clumps of *H. orientalis* by the front door have not been disturbed since Mr Honour came here – a proof of their longevity.

Folly Farm is a joy in spring, as the Astors discovered in 1951. There is a wonderful freshness, a feeling of anticipation, with the leaves on the lime trees showing pale green, and the fruit trees coming into full blossom.

Many of the shrubs and trees, chosen for their spring blossom, will give a vivid autumn display. Among the best on our alkaline (lime) soil the sorbus (mountain ash), the malus (apples) and pyrus (pears), with an underplanting of viburnums, berberis and choisya, will be spectacular each February. Have you remembered to plant scillas, muscari, chionodoxas and early narcissus under the deciduous shrubs?

It is at this moment of the year that I like to take in the structure of the garden. Emily Lucy Astor says it is divided into 'courts' (an abbreviation of 'courtyard', I think), rather than 'rooms', each one embracing the house as it is today. Hugh Astor has wisely extended the house wings, to make his library and drawing room larger, and to create a more sheltered place outside to sit and enjoy the sunshine. Discussing this, Hugh added with amusement that Lutyens was not always practical: originally he forgot the staircase here at Folly Farm, and he was reputed to have thought that a kitchen in the viceregal palace in New Delhi was unnecessary.

Lutyens' use of brickwork is outstanding in all the properties he designed – walls, steps and paths. Hugh says that the paths here are very much a part of the garden design: they create a geometric pattern with their mixture of stones, paving stones and herringbone brick. They have been here for the best part of ninety years and are now showing signs of wear and tear, so Hugh is repairing them over four or five years. The areas by the entrance and in front of the house have been done, and work on the sunken rose garden has been started. When that is complete, the paths around the canal will be tackled.

The yew hedges here are an important structural element, as they are at Great Dixter where the garden was also planned by Lutyens, in conjunction with the owner Nathaniel Lloyd. They create effective windbreaks and divisions between the 'courts', each with its individual mood. In the garden at Folly Farm there are considerable changes of level, but cleverly the tops of all the hedges are kept on the same horizontal plane. In the sunken rose garden they are 4.5 metres (15 ft) tall and elsewhere only about 2.5 metres (4 ft).

The hedges are cut in August, using electric clippers with a 90 cm (3 ft) blade, and scaffolding is needed to reach the top. To save the long job of clearing up, a sheet is laid along the bottom of the hedges to catch the clippings, which are sold for use in making cancer-cure drugs. Cutting starts after mid-August, and in good weather takes about three weeks (electric clippers cannot be used on wet days).

KIFTSGATE COURT

I love the garden at Kiftsgate in Gloucestershire – it is a garden for all seasons, perfected by the combined imaginations of three generations of inspired gardeners and the advice of a great designer. Major Lawrence Johnston of Hidcote Manor helped and advised his neighbour Mrs Muir when she was laying out the bones of the garden in the 1920s and 1930s.

Until Major Johnston came on the scene, there was only the paved garden in front of the portico. Then with his advice the now-existing steps from this formal garden by the house were added to give a convenient approach from the grass field. The next event was to expand the garden; to design the yellow border and make the rose border, and to plant yew and beech hedges. This has become the framework of the upper garden as it is today. In 1930, the daunting task of taming the steep, wooded bank and making a pathway down to the new 'lower garden' was undertaken, the work done with the help of Italian gardeners. There are incidents where visitors may pause – a lily pond on the way down, a small summer-house to rest in on the way up. This is an area with a completely different character and great planting possibility.

Graham Stuart Thomas, a critic to be followed, wrote of the whole garden in 1951: 'I regard this as the finest piece of skilled colour work that it has been my pleasure to see.' My own gardening mentor, Arthur Hellyer, wrote in 1954: 'Despite the luxuriance of Kiftsgate it is a garden upon which an extremely firm hand and a very discerning eye have been kept.' Forty years on, these words still ring true.

The early 1950s was the time when we in England were emerging from the years of 'utility' after the war. Once again we hoped to express our love of the pleasure of gardening. Diany Binney, Mrs Muir's daughter, was then guardian of the garden and kept the place going. Diany did not like to alter anything after her mother died, but fully realized that gardens will easily 'go back', especially after a hard winter. Plants must be replaced, shrubs and trees pruned. She made the semi-circular swimming pool in the lower garden and a ha-ha on the lawn at the bottom of the slope, and added a second path down the steep bank, lining it with variegated hollies. She also added the pool and well-head in the centre of the white garden, and two statues carved by Simon Verity.

Diany's other great contribution to this historic garden has been her endearing attitude, working in the garden even after handing over the property to her daughter, Anne Chambers. Visitors will catch her on her knees, weeding and tidying the borders, and she always notices essential jobs to be done.

The octagonal pool in the white garden was constructed in 1972. Diany saw the central feature – a well-head depicting the Four Seasons, a copy of the original made by a firm in the Pyrenees – at the Chelsea Flower Show. You can sit quite comfortably on the stone surround of the pool, studying

The planting in this border has a rhythm, using yellow flowers between purple-leaved acers and a strong contrast of leaf textures.

Variegated brunnera beside golden marjoram and variegated astrantia are a typical vignette. *Asphodeline lutea* and *Euphorbia myrsinites* contrast with mertensia in spring. The spires of lilies and *Hemerocallis* 'Golden Chimes', agapanthus and bronze phormium contrast with the rounded shapes of *Euphorbia characias*, rock roses and pale lemon hypericum. Another good combination is *Heuchera cylindrica* 'Greenfinch' with lemon balm and blue anchusa. *Rosa* 'Graham Thomas' is 2.1 metres (7 ft) tall under one of the acers, with *Ligularia dentata* 'Desdemona' nearby.

The border here displays the sure mastery of Anne's and her mother's planting. ❧

OVERLEAF The garden at Kiftsgate is open from 1 April until the end of September. In April you will catch the beauty of the naturalized bluebells growing in the wood on the south side of the house – on your left as you arrive. Every moment in this garden has its own beauty, and the dryopteris ferns interspersed with the bluebells give an element of freshness. Both ferns and bluebells love dappled shade and have been growing and increasing here for years. A few bluebells, *Endymion non-scripta* (in your autumn bulb catalogues), planted this year will develop into a blue carpet for your grandchildren. ❧

the intricate carving, enjoying the sound of the water – but watch which way the wind is blowing, so the spray will not reach you. Sit for a while and ponder. I did so on a July day in 1995, and discovered Diany on her knees clearing dead tulip stems from under a philadelphus.

Camellias do not like the alkaline soil of Gloucestershire, but at Kiftsgate they have succeeded with *C. cuspidata*, a native of west China, introduced by E. H. Wilson in 1900; it is covered with tiny white flowers in March and April. Ernest Wilson was a native of Chipping Campden, close to Hidcote and Kiftsgate, and I feel sure he must have been a gardening friend of Lawrence Johnston. Another of his introductions from China, in 1908, was *Stachyurus chinensis*. The wide-spreading specimen growing at Kiftsgate is an important feature of the driveway planting. There are quantities of narcissus naturalized here and in the bluebell wood. The *Fritillaria meleagris* open in April, and to ensure that these will increase, you must allow their seeds to ripen and fall before mowing.

Anne's first choice among indispensable spring plants is *Brunnera macrophylla* 'Variegata'. As she wrote in the gardening quarterly *Hortus*, it is a 'top-class spring plant. It has lovely heart-shaped, cream-edged leaves with an azure blue forget-me-not flower.' These leaves brighten the border before herbaceous plants take over. (At Barnsley we grow it in semi-shade

*T*he garden captures the freshness of spring with a planting of *Tulipa* 'Triumphator' grouped under *Viburnum × carlcephalum*.

Notice how the steps with their shallow risers make an uphill journey seem easy. On the right the pine trunks add a vertical accent, and behind is the winter-flowering *Prunus incisa* 'Praecox'.

and are propagating it by offsets from the parent plant.) An early spring star in the lower garden is the pea, *Lathyrus vernus*. The purple/blue variety is easiest: not only do clumps increase in size, but it will also seed itself, so take care not to weed out the seedlings. This form and *L. v. roseus* are definitely 'front-of-the-border' plants for spring attraction.

Under deciduous trees is a good place to establish a display of bulbs and other early treasures, to be enjoyed before the leaves open. Although erythroniums (dog's-tooth violets), trilliums and sanguinaria do not like limy soil, Anne has discovered that they will survive at Kiftsgate but not 'take off' as they would in an acid woodland soil. Corydalis, on the other hand, loves our limestone, and these four now grow under a *Staphylea colchica*, the bladder nut. This remarkable shrub is growing by the living-room window at Kiftsgate and provides pleasure all through the year. The leaves, oblong with a shiny green under-surface, open in April, and are followed by panicles of creamy-white flowers, covering the tree in early May. Anne finds their distinctive smell reminiscent of coconut ice-cream, and they combine well with other white-flowered shrubs in the sunken garden.

Spring is a time to pause in the garden and focus on detail. The acid-yellow flowers of the acers *A. aconitifolium* and *A. griseum,* now coming into leaf, demand your attention. The pink flowers of the golden-leaved *Ribes sanguineum* 'Brocklebankii' open now. Like many shrubs with golden foliage, it is happier out of direct sunlight so the leaves do not become scorched in high summer.

Visit Kiftsgate at every season, to stimulate your imagination and discover new plants. The garden is open to the public from 1 April until the end of September but do check times and days before going there. You will appreciate it more if you take time to read the guidebook and the list of plants growing in each area of the garden. I always bring my own notebook so I can write the names of special plants I have admired and would like to have in our garden at Barnsley. You will find that many are available to take home with you.

How easy it is for a great garden to become overgrown, a forgotten secret, if those who succeed its maker have not the inspiration, imagination, time and dedication to devote to its upkeep. Fortunately, three remarkable generations have prevented this from happening at Kiftsgate – and we in the late 1990s can reap the benefit, deriving enjoyment, inspiration, and ideas for our own gardens, large or small.

Kiftsgate is a family garden, conceived and cared for by ladies of strong character, all with a deep horticultural knowledge and close affinity with the soil. Anne Chambers, the third generation here, has brought a freshness appropriate to the late twentieth century. This is what the English country garden is all about.

BARNSLEY HOUSE

*T*his house was built in 1697 by Brereton Bourchier, the squire of Barnsley, and from the mid eighteenth century it was The Rectory. My father-in-law bought the property in 1939 and changed its name to 'The Close' – called after the adjoining paddock. He gave the house to David, my late husband, in 1951, and we moved in on 4 March with our four children – it was exciting for all of us. We changed the name to Barnsley House, converted the old stables and coach house into a home for my father- and mother-in-law and called this 'The Close'. So it remained for forty-five years. I now live on my own in 'The Close' and am fortunate still to be able to oversee the running of the garden.

I am often asked, 'What was the garden like when you came here?' It was suffering from the understaffing of the war years, but had beautiful features from past centuries.

The wall built on three sides in 1770 ends in a north-facing Gothic Survival alcove, there are trees more than a hundred years old, yew hedges and box planted in the nineteenth century. Best of all was the soil, which in places had been cultivated for generations.

David and I grassed over an existing border facing north-west under the long wall – it was too dry and sunless. Twin perennial borders backed with yew hedges went also, to create a large open space for tree planting; later we called this 'the wilderness'. One yew hedge we turned round to enclose the swimming pool, and the other we moved to run at right angles from the summer-house. We kept the fastigiate yew trees (now large and fat) flanking the crazy paving path, as a main axis from the house.

The cross-axis running parallel to the wall happened almost by chance. David was given the 1770 Tuscan temple from Fairford Park. This now fits snugly between the walls of the pond garden and is the making of the garden. From there a perfect vista, a wide grass path, leads to the stone fountain carved by Simon Verity in 1972.

We planted the first trees in the lime avenue in 1954, and later added more. In 1964, the year of our twenty-fifth wedding anniversary, my brother Francis and his wife gave us fourteen laburnums to make into a tunnel. This is an important feature, both in May underplanted with red tulips, and in June when the laburnum is in flower with a sea of *Allium aflatunense* underneath.

The knot garden, the herb bed and the decorative potager were all made in the 1970s, much influenced by reading seventeenth-century books, as I feel the designs complement the house.

My aim is to make the beds as full of colour as possible right through from March to autumn. They start with mauve, yellow and white – crocus, narcissus and hellebores – then some are taken over with white, yellow and orange tulips, and others with red tulips, all underplanted with forget-me-nots, cowslips and primulas. As the bulbs fade, perennial leaves of hostas,

*T*he dark fastigiate yews planted in 1946 each side of the crazy paving path line the way to the south-east side of the house, where the original front door has the date-stone 1697 above and the initials B.B. The contrast of the dark yew with the pale colour of the limestone is dramatic, especially in early morning light. The house, built by Brereton Bourchier, has a continuous drip-mould above the lower windows and individual drip-moulds were added above each dormer in 1830. They give firm horizontal lines and character to the house.

The rock roses, an important feature, are in flower from late May through June. Hardy geraniums and wild strawberries have seeded themselves through the paving, giving more colour.

delphiniums, monardas, polemonium grow up and hide the bulb leaves, so we can allow most of them to remain to flower next year.

For these three months of the year there will always be a new surprise in the garden. As the early species crocus die off there will be others to replace them. The large Dutch crocus will change the colour in our borders from mauve to white, and then the first narcissus will be opening. We will see the results of our autumn bulb planting as the tulips come through and open. Among my favourites are *T*. 'Prinses Irene', lily-flowered 'White Triumphator' and 'Mariette'.

March rain is often gentle, just right to slowly moisten the borders. Spring to me is golden; from there colours develop and we can appreciate how some are in harmony and others in contrast. Daffodils are often a strident yellow and need to be quietened down, so how do we do this? There are groups of honesty – a strong purple – and pale narcissus.

The last two weeks in May are always rather difficult – and that is when visitors come from the United States and Europe to visit us, and to see the Chelsea Flower Show. Most of the tulips are over and so are the flowering

I like to stand, at any time of the day, and enjoy the view of the Tuscan temple. My husband David brought it to Barnsley in 1962 from Fairford Park, where it was built as an eye-catcher in 1770. Now it is a major feature in our garden, surrounded on three sides by our wall of the same date.

Sitting in the temple, you have a vista towards the frog fountain, and in the evenings the swallows and bats fly around, catching flies, swooping over the water. The temple is reflected in the dark water, and on sunny days ripples light up and dance on the white back wall. *Phormium tenax*, New Zealand flax, frame the picture, and the narrow beds around the pool are planted with kingcups, primulas and blue *Iris sibirica*.

cherries and crab apples; everything is full of expectancy and promise, including the roses. Under the skirt of branches of the two weeping cherries, *Prunus × yedoensis* 'Perpendens', just before their leaves open, is a ground-cover of yellow *Erythronium* 'Pagoda'.

Nature, always clever, has her own way of displaying flowers to their best advantage. Have you noticed how the earliest flowers are low – snowdrops, aconites, crocus, anemones, pulmonarias, polyanthus – and they are succeeded by taller varieties – daffodils, tulips, wallflowers and forget-me-nots? When these are over the shrubs are in full foliage, and then the leaves on deciduous trees open and cast their shade. This is a vertical panorama, both in space and in time.

*T*he camera can catch moments which we may miss. In spring, yellow tulips are massed through the dark purple honesty, *Lunaria annua*. Standard shrubs are useful to allow more space for underplanting, and here I have used the weeping *Caranga arborescens* 'Pendula'. The pea-shaped yellow flowers open along the hanging branchlets in May. It is a useful shrub, growing in poor soil and on a windy site.

In the background two fastigiate yews contrast well with the rounded, clipped hollies, *Ilex × altaclerensis* 'Golden King', and the snowberry, *Symphoricarpos orbiculatus* 'Foliis Variegatis'.

SUMMER

We all look forward to high summer when the borders have a feeling of luxuriance and the vegetables are prolific. Everything will be growing apace and some of the taller perennials need staking. There should be no bare earth as half-hardies like penstemon, diascias, lobelias and white daisies, *Argyranthemum frutescens*, have been put out into the spaces where tulips have been taken up among the perennial hardy geraniums, poppies, campanulas, *Hesperis matronalis*, delphiniums and monardas.

All kinds of roses are in bloom, scenting the summer air and waiting to be picked for indoor arrangements. Every day dead-heading is important; as well as the roses the annuals and perennials must be taken care of to keep a succession of fresh flowers opening.

The 'stand-by' shrubs, deutzias, philadelphus, kolkwitzias and weigelas help to give substance to mixed borders, and these will need their summer pruning in August.

With his artistic skill, John Hubbard has combined structure, plants and ceramics at Chilcombe House. His aim is to create a luxuriant picture in such a way that he has time both for painting and planting, and the effect is a tapestry of muted colours. In this photograph foxgloves mingle with poppies, angelica, pulmonaria and white saxifrage in the foreground. The line of clipped box structures the scene, and shady places become important. Welsh poppies are allowed to seed themselves, adding a splash of yellow and orange. The plant with the spotted leaf is pulmonaria.

CHILCOMBE HOUSE

*J*ohn Hubbard and his wife Caryl discovered Chilcombe after driving along bumpy tracks and across fields to reach this old farmhouse in its ideal situation in Hardy's Wessex, where buzzards still hang on the air. They wondered, were they prepared to spend time and energy on this beautiful but ramshackle house with its overgrown garden? They moved in in 1969 and now Chilcombe is a Mecca for gardeners, garden historians, and those who appreciate colour co-ordination, intimate design and a garden overflowing with plants in a comparatively small space.

Surrounded by old walls on a south-east-facing slope, the main garden is carefully crafted. John and Caryl did not sit down with pencil and paper, as I would have expected artistic people to do. They went straight into the garden and planned out the hedges and divisions to create compartments, using string and bamboos. The paths, some original but mostly new, create vistas leading from one area to the next; some run direct from the north-west boundary wall and others at right angles, so creating cross-vistas. The hedges now give height as do the arches they planned, and the fastigiate trees they soon planted.

'We stay indoors in winter,' John told me, and this in no way surprised me. He, an artist, is kept busy in his studio, and Caryl his wife is occupied with her own work in the art world.

We avoid April too, because of the winds and general disagreeableness of being fairly exposed at a tricky time. We have tulips and other early plants in the beds we can see from the house, and a lot of things on the raised banks to the north, beside our driveway and the entrance to our house, so inevitably we see them most days. There are aconites, cyclamen, quantities of snowdrops and white daffodils mixed with yellow doronicums; also mixed hellebores which we can look up to.

As most hellebores hang their heads, the ideal site for them is above your eye level so you can see into their wonderful faces.

You do not have to walk in your garden when the weather is against you – you can appreciate it from your desk, your bedroom or kitchen windows. Chilcombe, with its stormy wind from the sea, is a garden like this: 31.5 metres (105 ft) above sea level and 1.6 km (1 mile) only from the coast, it is affected throughout the year by its closeness to the Channel. Searing winds come from the south-east in the spring, often laden with salt air, and even during summer chilling sea-fogs sometimes drift in. On the plus side, the soil is neutral to alkaline with patches of greensand, and the view looking towards the south is breathtakingly beautiful; over the wall the fields roll on towards the chalk downs.

By May plants are burgeoning into growth and the Hubbards are once more at work in their garden. John emphasizes the difference between painting a picture on canvas and creating living garden pictures. Painting

*L*ooking from the walled garden towards the old farmhouse, through a massed planting of purple, red, white and different greens. Sweet peas trained on bamboos echo the shape of the box pyramids and contrast with the horizontal box edging.

The combination of structure and luxuriance of planting is outstanding. It has a cottage-garden style with the subtle knowledge of a plantsman and John's artist's eye. Divided into garden rooms, Chilcombe reminds me of twentieth-century Hidcote but also of the seventeenth-century clergyman, William Lawson, and his idea of the perfect form of a garden.

The planting here includes *Penstemon heterophyllus*, *Salvia microphylla*, potentilla, centaurea, hedysarum and iris.

requires training and natural skill to create a picture using the tools of the trade; the painter is in complete control. Creating a garden or just designing a successful border requires both an understanding of plants, and imagination. Whereas the painter sees the result of his work immediately in front of him on his easel, the gardener often has to wait weeks, months, or even years before his flowers bloom or his trees reach maturity, and he is dependent on the quality of the plants, his soil and the weather.

A picture on canvas is a static work of art; once painted, it is only altered by its frame and the aspect of the wall on which it is hung, and it can be enjoyed for centuries. At this moment I look at an oil painting by Victoria Rees given to me in 1990 of our laburnum tunnel, and above it is *Arum*

maximum Aegyptiacum painted on vellum in 1760: I must stand in front of them to enjoy them fully. In contrast, as you walk along your border, your view changes with every step – in a way it is like a moving picture. John and Caryl appreciate this, and have interpreted the twin artistic skills of the painter and the gardener in a highly successful way.

The old walls built of local Swyre stone indicate that a thoroughly useful farmhouse garden has been cultivated here for centuries, vegetables, herbs and fruit probably predominating. John and Caryl have brought their own ideas, sophisticated and artistic to change and enhance it.

If you arrive on a still day, as I did, the climate is deceptive, for the shelter-belt trees planted by the Hubbards twenty-five years ago give protection from the north and west. In the farmyard a mature gean, *Prunus avium,* a spreading fig, an American walnut and a climbing hydrangea all help to coax you into a feeling of calm, while the small church, with a Norman nave, chancel and font, completes the protection from the east.

From the farmyard, a doorway in an old wall leads into a small enclosed court, where my attention was immediately drawn to an unusual climbing plant growing in a large pot beside the fifteenth-century door. It is *Sollya fusiformis* from New Zealand, with pure blue lantern-like flowers.

RIGHT *C*aryl has charge of the vegetables, but allows flowers to grow amidst them to add extra colour. Straight lines of lettuce, spinach, radishes and leeks are bounded by stone edging and paths.

The planting here is on a small scale, yielding enough for a family of two. The standards are gooseberries, and hibiscus, one blue and one pink; one is to be changed so there will be a matching pair. The tall grey plant is onopordum, and *Diascia nigrescens* form a spectacular line of pink. It is the combination of formal and informal that gives the whole garden its magic.

LEFT *S*ummer in the sundial garden – a quiet space in the walled garden on this south-facing slope. The sundial is surrounded by polygonum, alliums and lawn, and defined on one side by narrow beds of 'Hidcote' lavender, on another by taller perennials, including *Campanula alliariifolia*, francoa and *Verbascum chaixii* 'Album'. Beside the crazy paving path there are penstemons and *Convolvulus cneorum*.

Throughout the garden, a series of arches gives extra height and the opportunity to grow climbers, roses and clematis. Here, on one corner, *Rosa* 'Canary Bird' flowers in June and July; the red rose in the left foreground has now been replaced by *Ozothamnus rosmarinifolius*.

It was exciting for the Hubbards when they first dug down through a foot or more of soil and discovered that this yard was paved with old cobbles, which they immediately uncovered. The pattern of paths is now quite informal and I felt free to browse – remember it is a small area – and enjoy all the low-growing and ground-cover plants, many self-seeded in the cracks of the cobbles: wild strawberries, *Stachys lanata,* aubrieta, ladies' mantle and snow-in-summer. The forget-me-nots had finished flowering but had re-sown for next year, and so had the yellow Welsh poppies and feverfew. Welsh poppies, once you have them, are friendly plants. They will germinate and take over any corner or crack in the paving that is available; equally, the seedlings can be easily taken out. At Barnsley we now have single and double yellow and orange plants – almost everywhere. Visitors imagine that I am being extremely generous when I give them a ripe seed head with an ample supply of seed to set their garden aglow next May. *Buddleja lindleyana, Hydrangea villosa* and both white and pink jasmine were flowering, astrantia and sweet cecily adding height beside a variegated dogwood. Then there were the tender plants, some in pots – many verbenas, salvias, fuchsias, penstemons and lobelias.

Another arch in the wall leads you to the south-east side of the house. This is the most relaxing part of the garden, with its peaceful lawn and Portland stone shell fountain, where one of the Hubbards' terriers will always perform, wallowing in the shallow water, splashing and smiling to draw your attention. You can sit and watch him from a nearby seat.

Here on this side of the house is the original front door, with elegant steps and railings and narrow borders each side. I was full of admiration for the planting – a pair of deciduous *Ceanothus* 'Henri Desfossé', with violet blue flowers in midsummer, and three well-established *Bupleurum fruticosum,* described in Hillier's manual as 'one of the best evergreen shrubs for exposed places near the sea'. For grey leaves there are *Dorycnium hirsutum (Lotus hirsutus)* and cistus, the white, tinged pink flowers of the dorycnium in pretty contrast to the flowers of *Caryopteris* × *clandonensis* 'Kew Blue'. These borders have a feeling of well-being, and are the perfect foil for this side of the house.

Another narrow border on the other side of the lawn and opposite the front door runs under the enclosing wall of the main garden. Here two Florence Court yews, *Taxus* 'Fastigiata', planted several decades ago, rather block the view but must break the force of the wind. The wall is only 1.2 metres (4 ft) high this side, so looking over it you have an exciting view across the walled garden into the unspoilt

Dorset countryside. The border, also only 1.2 metres (4 ft) wide, is thickly planted with penstemons, *Salvia verticillata*, hostas, euphorbias, calamintha, *Solanum rantonnetii* and *Viola cornuta*.

Now at last we can step down into the walled garden. John and Caryl have terraced and divided the south-east-facing slope enclosed by the old walls, creating small garden rooms (John calls them areas) with carefully espaliered pears, trained clematis, a narrow path with hedges of green and purple yew, beech and holly. Mown grass, brick and cobble paths help to establish geometric patterns throughout the garden, but first you should turn right and walk slowly along the inside of the wall, for it is covered with clematis, honeysuckles and roses galore.

Caryl is responsible for the herb and vegetable garden, at the lower end of the slope, below the formal calm of the sundial garden and the beech and holly alley. The pathway takes you into the potager where salads, peas and beans, cabbages and leeks bear witness to her industry. Ruby chard, chicory and lettuces in variety add an artistry to the vegetables. These are intermingled with lobelias, parsley and sage. It is a perfect association of colour, vegetables, herbs and flowers. Everything is in harmony, the paths, narrow but useful, taking you between a bright yellow *Oenothera* 'Lady Brookborough', grey-leaved senecio and *Eryngium giganteum*. Caryl works hard planning her summer vegetables, sowing seeds for her salads and keeping the weeds at bay.

Throughout the day I spent with John and Caryl, my thoughts kept turning like a magnet back to historic Dorset, and to Tudor gardens. In AD 43/44 Vespasian, commanding the Second Augustan Legion, fought his way through the county. Did they march across Chilcombe's rolling pastures? And, as often happens when I visit an old house, William Lawson came to mind, one of my favourite early seventeenth-century characters, who wrote so engagingly to help the country housewife to grow vegetables and herbs and to save her own seeds; he also taught her husband how to graft fruit trees – apples, pears, cherries, damsons and filberts – a fashionable art in the seventeenth century, and an old orchard in the walled garden still flowers and fruits in due season. Lawson's advice is characteristically full of common sense: 'I advise the Mistress either to be present herself, or to teach her maids to know herbs from weeds'; and 'The Gardner had not need be an idle or lazy Lubber . . . there will ever be something to do.' John and Caryl, who do much of the gardening themselves, will endorse this.

In its present form Chilcombe, unlike Dixter, Helmingham and Holker, is a recently developed garden. But the whole place has an enchantment: the narrow paths (I had to take John's arm to negotiate some of them), the unexpected corners and vistas, the colour combinations, always in harmony. It has become the epitome of the true English country garden – beautiful and dearly loved by its owners, and also by many in the gardening world.

Still in the walled garden, after walking through the sundial garden and down narrow, precipitous steps, you reach another small area with a generosity of planting. Here as elsewhere every opportunity is used, and there is scarcely a square inch of soil showing. This helps to retain moisture during dry summers.

On the left, the bank is covered with many varieties of thyme – white, mauve, pink, and with grey as well as green leaves. This is an especially scented moment, walking along the paved path edged on the right with lavender, sage, penstemons, *Convolvulus cneorum* and origanum.

HOLKER HALL

We all love our gardens in June when the roses are at their best, peas, beans and salad crops are plentiful, and strawberries lusciously ripe. My visit to Holker in Cumbria during the last week in June 1995 provided all these bounties and was also a typical example of the vagaries of our English weather. Whatever do I tell American visitors when they ring me from the States to ask, What is the best month for our visit to England? Do we need warm or cool clothes? and Will it be raining? Who knows?

I flew to Holker, piloted by my friend Anne Norman in her four-seater Robin, landing at Cark to find the sun shining, the sky blue with intermittent white clouds – a perfect day for a garden visit. There had been a strong headwind, so our somewhat bumpy flight had taken longer than expected. This did not matter, as I could enjoy the aerial views of sprawling towns spreading into the English countryside, and the grand estates with their surrounding unspoilt acres and old trees. Sometimes the avenues leading to historic houses were predominant; more frequent were the golf courses which now pepper the landscape.

The next day, strong winds blew up in Gloucestershire. The clouds were low, visibility was poor, and it was not safe for Anne's aircraft to take off to come and fetch me. The contrast with the day before was dramatic – it was hard to believe the sudden change, and I would find it difficult to explain to American friends unless they live in a hurricane area.

Holker, close by the sea, near Grange-over-Sands, is protected by a warm westerly airstream, and only seldom has to contend with severe frosts. The average annual rainfall is 150 cm (60 in). The natural pH in the woodland area is probably 5.3, but in the flower garden, where leaf mould, farmyard manure and slow-release fertilizers are used as a mulch in autumn and a boost in spring on all the borders, the average pH, when analysed, was 6.5. Many of the most successful shrubs and trees in the woodland are acid-loving: rhododendrons, azaleas, stewartias, magnolias and hundreds of

Grania is full of original ideas. Here on the right she is using standard *Prunus lusitanica* as an avenue, their leading branches trained to make a shady archway. I am looking forward to using this idea.

This summer garden is especially designed for visitors who can stroll around, take notes or sit on a seat on summer afternoons while the younger generation walks further afield. My impressions are of symmetry, Edwardian urns, upright yews and the English lawn surrounded by blue and white perennials, red roses, blue delphiniums – a restful colour scheme.

others. When plants needing an alkaline soil are put in, building rubble containing lime is mixed into the ground.

I was interested to find that the plants in this garden, owned by Hugh and Grania Cavendish, were probably two weeks ahead of ours at Barnsley House. Hugh explained to me how, being further north, they have longer hours of daylight than we do, from late spring through to early autumn, which encourages plants that need a long day to flower.

Hugh and Grania are the perfect husband-and-wife team. Both have tremendous enthusiasm, talent and energy, but it is their love of Holker which enables them to face undaunted the unending task of keeping everything here vital and renewed. Starting a new garden requires imagination, money and energy, but to keep an old garden *à point* needs love and sustained work. Holker, although open to the public, is still essentially a home for the family. Hugh and Grania both love the whole garden, and while Grania, with her discerning eye, plans the border planting and colour schemes, Hugh gives his heart to the trees and shrubs in the extensive arboretum.

*T*he evening light playing on the formal planting in the summer garden. Grania has planned this to be especially restful and interesting for summer visitors, so they can sit quietly and enjoy the shadows, the design of the curving box edging and the lawn, with the house in the background. The grey *Pyrus salicifolia*, grown as standards, make a lighter impact. It is a reminder of the importance of green. The structure of this garden could be copied on a smaller scale in a town garden.

Hugh grew up at Holker, and his grandmother, Lady Moyra Cavendish, inspired him and sowed the seed of gardening in his mind, as well as an understanding of the property. As Hugh and I walked through the woodland he told me a little about the history of the estate.

Lady Elizabeth Cavendish and her husband, Sir Thomas Lowther, the owners in 1720, created formal gardens in the fashionable Dutch style, with clipped and topiaried hedges – all transported by ship from London. Imagine the excitement as these were off-loaded, and the family and staff watched their placement around the house, together with statues for focal points and to stand in the niches in the hedges. The hedges had time to mature and the statues grew lichened – I wish plans or paintings had been made of this garden before it was swept away by Lord George Cavendish sixty years later.

Lord George was a godson of King George II and very involved with the Royal Household, so it was quite natural that he should be abreast with the times, and familiar with the new ideas of the landscape movement, brought back from Europe by home-coming Grand Tourists. A 'contrived natural landscape' should be the view from their windows, not a formal Dutch garden. Lord George was a keen, gifted and knowledgeable gardener, and as Hugh and I walked round we saw trees his ancestor had planted, including the Cedar of Lebanon grown from seed sent to him by a friend from the Middle East. Lord George's shrubs and trees flourished and matured, and then a half-century later Lord Burlington, son of the Duke of Devonshire, consulted Joseph Paxton (head gardener at Chatsworth), and more work was carried out, enlarging the garden, making an arboretum, a walled kitchen garden and a fountain.

There has always been a family continuity at Holker, and from 1908 Lady Moyra Cavendish, often quoted as the architect of the gardens, improved, altered and added to the existing gardens. She and her husband, Lord Richard, sought advice from the fashionable designer of the day, Thomas Mawson. He envisaged and made the rose garden some distance from the house – recently extended and replanted by Hugh and Grania. He also laid out a new garden outside the library. This was labour-intensive, with seasonal bedding; labour was cheap, and work was found for some thirteen gardeners. Grania and Hugh realize that change is important, at the same time respecting what has been handed down to them.

Now visitors begin their tour of the garden through a gate leading into this garden. Grania has cleverly replanned it in shape and planting and, no longer relying on bedding-out, there is still colour and interest from springtime until autumn. Four beds are designed to wrap round a central ellipse (hence its name, the elliptical garden); shelter is given on one side by pleached limes and there is a lovely view across the park. The paths, which are edged in cobbles and slate, are made of hoggin, a crushed limestone put down when it is wet, and rolled; it is weed-proof and easy to walk on all the year,

Here there are four slate seats, all individually cut to fit the ellipse and each flanked by two standard *Hydrangea paniculata* 'Grandiflora' and backed by yew hedges and *Nepeta* 'Six Hills Giant'. Choose one to sit on and quietly read the brochure so you will know what plants to look out for.

The four sections of the garden are planted by colour: pink, yellow, purples and deep reds and lilac, all with blue and white infilling. The central paths are edged with *Lavandula dentata*. Delphiniums in hazel cages, eight varieties of differently shaped box, clipped yews and ilex, all add architecture amid the tumbling shrubs and herbaceous plants. There are several philadelphus, and the buddlejas include *B. alternifolia* 'Argentea', *B. davidii* 'Empire Blue' and *B. d.* 'White Bouquet'.

Other shrubs for height and colour include *Olearia stellulata*, *Deutzia* × *hybrida* 'Magicien', *Indigofera dielsiana* and *I. heterantha*. These are interplanted with perennials – the Russian mallow *Alcea rugosa*, *Crambe cordifolia*, *Baptisia australis*, several penstemons, *Veronica* 'Snowgiant', *Hemerocallis* 'Catherine Woodbery', *Agastache foeniculum*, *Anemone multifida* and others. *Regale* lilies, blue and white agapanthus, nerines and phlox do well here. The roses chosen by Grania are 'Madame Hardy', 'Président de Sèze', 'Général Kléber', 'Madame Legras de Saint Germain', 'Nuits de Young', 'La Ville de Bruxelles', 'Capitaine John Ingram', and 'Mary Queen of Scots'.

The climbers match the scale of the house, and the planting against it has been carefully thought out. Here there is an opportunity to use tender plants which many of us cannot grow outside all through the year. On the corner by the visitors' entrance gate is the white *Abutilon vitifolium* 'Tennant's White' and the anemone rose, *Rosa anemoneflora,* both susceptible to frost. They are hardy here where frosts are infrequent, and were both flowering in late June.

A loquat, *Eriobotrya japonica,* and a white solanum were happy beside *Magnolia grandiflora* 'Goliath' and the white-flowered *Buddleja salviifolia*. There were agapanthus in flower and the unusual *Bowkeria citrina*, a South African plant the Cavendishes have grown from seed. *Cistus* 'Silver Pink' and *Lavandula stoechas* complete the picture.

Planting on and under the other south-facing wall of the house – quite protected from the wind – includes the Banksian rose and a *Ceanothus arboreus* 'Trewithen Blue'. The exciting *Solanum laciniatum* or kangaroo apple grows well here, proclaiming the absence of frosts in recent years. There is a good specimen of *Daphne bholua*, grown from seed given to Hugh by Sir Peter Smithers. Once well established this Himalayan shrub is quite hardy and produces wonderful scented flowers during January and February.

*I*f you are fortunate enough to meet Grania Cavendish, you will see that she is as beautiful as her elliptical garden. Thomas Mawson designed this a hundred years ago, and Grania has updated it, so that when you walk through the white gate a whole panorama unfolds itself, no longer relying on bedding-out. The central feature is an ellipse – hence its name – where you can rest on four slate seats. The beds around are filled with nepeta, delphiniums, anthemis, annual sweet peas, monardas – the colours we all love in combination. Grania keeps off strident reds except for *Tropaeolum speciosum*.

Turn the corner to look at the bed on the west-facing wall of the house, and you will find an underplanting of sarcococca, hebes, parahebe, ballota, potentillas. Taller shrubs include *Azara microphylla,* viburnums, *Itea ilicifolia,* philadelphus, hydrangeas – all to complement the climbers, *Schizophragma hydrangeoïdes* and roses, including *R. gigantea* (Cooper's Burmese) and *R. banksiae* 'Lutea', both reaching up to the gables.

In the private garden, where the family can relax without being overlooked by the public, Grania has made an oasis surrounded by borders, using shrubs and perennials we think of as high-summer plants – roses, delphiniums, white potentillas, monkshood, philadelphus and crambe. The central lawn is large enough for family croquet – the tennis court is elsewhere.

The long border on the other side, backed by beech hedges, has viburnums still in flower, lilies coming into flower through apricot digitalis, golden marjoram and rue for foliage effect, *Hebe* 'Mrs Winder' and hardy geraniums. It is deceptively simple, with a romantic cottage-garden feeling, as though the owners had just put together a collection of plants – but all are chosen to give the maximum effect. This is the ultimate skill of gardeners: knowing what plants will flower with harmonious neighbours.

Buddlejas are clipped, some low and others at 1–1.25 metres (3–4 ft) to give extra height and a change of rhythm along the borders. There are standard *Hydrangea paniculata* 'Grandiflora', with squares of box edging surrounding them to make them more important. The estate carpenter has made arches for clematis and roses to clamber through, and metal pyramids for honeysuckles.

Large Versailles tubs stand by the loggia. In summer these are filled with a variety of sweet peas, creating a lively tapestry of colour. For unobtrusive supports they have hazel twigs, bent over and tied at the top; the same device is used to stake the tall delphiniums in the borders. Large terracotta containers have permanent planting, with clipped holly and bay trees.

Every detail in the garden is so carefully carried out – the clipping, the pruning, the plant infilling, and the patterns and paving. On the terrace immediately under the west-facing side of the house is a simple knot garden, made with box and santolina. This mixture of the formal with the informal gives the garden a very relaxed feeling.

Visitors go down stone steps from the elliptical garden into the summer garden. On their right is a wooden pergola supporting trained 'Lord Lambourne' apples and pears, lovely in spring blossom and in autumn with the ripening fruit. Here in the summer garden the design is formal, with paths wide enough to allow visitors to walk comfortably without feeling crowded. The lawn is well kept – remember the annual 150 cm (60 in) of rain. The central path has a clever planting I have not seen elsewhere: standard Portugal laurels, *Prunus lusitanica,* form an avenue, their leading

Grania is a practical gardener and full of ideas. She and Hugh have planned their garden so that there are quiet, private places for themselves and their family where they can sit, walk and play croquet undisturbed by the public who wander in the rest of the garden.

Leading away from their loggia, paths are flanked by pots with evergreen bays and summer-flowering sweet peas supported by hazel twigs, bent over and tied above in the container. Grania's beds are full with perennials – lupins, peonies, diascias, delphiniums, digitalis and cascades of roses. Buddlejas are pruned to varying heights and *Crambe cordifolia* has its tall, airy flowers. The scale is all-important with the walls of the house.

branches trained up and over to make an archway. These are trees which clip well, and in a few years they will make an exciting tunnel. The path leads right through to the end of this garden and a fine wrought-iron gate through which you can see the wild-flower meadow, and beyond it a large bowl-shaped slate sundial.

In the centre of the summer garden is a circular path containing four beds, box-edged, with weeping silver pear trees, *Pyrus salicifolia,* underplanted with a mixture of spring bulbs, later replaced with ornamental cabbages or echiums, providing colour from April to October. The outer circle is edged with clipped *Teucrium chamaedrys,* all originating from four plants brought back from Barnsley some years ago. The beds flanking the other walks are full of herbaceous plants, small shrubs and bulbs, given structure by box squares containing clipped *Crataegus orientalis.*

Among the roses are 'Gipsy Boy', 'Great Maiden's Blush', 'Châpeau de Napoléon' and the long-flowering *Rosa mutabilis,* all underplanted with nepeta, alliums, geraniums and a wide variety of double primroses and spring bulbs. Visitors love 'a riot of colour' and, as Grania says, this is a lovely spot for the more elderly visitors to sit while the young members of the family go off and explore the woodland.

Holker Hall Garden won the Christie/Historic Houses' Association 'Garden of the Year' Award in 1994, and rightly so. If I lived closer I would buy a season ticket and try to visit at least once a month, bringing my notebook and my camera. There is always something new happening – new plants, new trees and new ideas.

Grania and Hugh have recently been to see gardens in Devon and Cornwall, bringing home a good carload of plants – all suitable for their almost frost-free climate. Most of these have either been put into a nursery bed or are lined out by the greenhouse, where an eye can be kept on them throughout summer. They will be put into their permanent homes during the autumn re-arrangements in the borders and the woodland. To keep the borders alive, it is vitally important to visit nurseries and buy new plants. We must also remember to pass on cuttings of treasures to our neighbours and gardening friends who will nurture them and give them back if we lose the original.

Strolling alone through the summer and private gardens in the evening, I absorbed their beauty with the house as a backdrop, the evening light playing on the warm pink of the stone and the glistening glass windows. (Most of them still have their old glass, which with its uneven surface reflects the light more subtly than our modern glass.) White clouds were moving fast above the silhouette of the house and the arboretum, contrasting with the spires of the evergreens and the bosoms of the deciduous trees. Similar thoughts must have caught Hugh's imagination as he was growing up, just as they caught mine on that June afternoon.

*I*f you follow either of the walks (see page 120) you reach the rose garden originally designed by Thomas Mawson, now enlarged to include water (the pool was built by estate labour in 1988) and replanted with imagination by Grania and Hugh to suit our more informal twentieth-century taste. It is a good resting place to sit and absorb what you have already seen, and appreciate the scents while making notes about the unusual shrubs and climbers which have been introduced to this sheltered area. On the wall a dunalia, native of South America, has 5 cm (2 in) long, bluish-purple bell-shaped flowers, and also in the Solanaceae family is *Solanum crispum* 'Variegatum'.

The two gazebos, made locally, are supports for climbing roses and honeysuckles. Hugh's slate quarries provide the limestone and blue-black slate for material for the seats.

HELMINGHAM HALL

*T*he new rose garden at Helmingham was looking perfect at the end of June. You see it first from the raised grass walk looking over the knot and herb garden with a stone statue of Flora as its central feature.

This was laid out in 1982 and dividing the knots from the rose garden are two rectangular beds, long and narrow, each with fifteen 'Rosa Mundi' (*R. gallica* 'Versicolor') bushes, edged with catmint, and underplanted with forget-me-nots which re-seed themselves each year.

Xa Tollemache is considering what to plant to give interest after the once-flowering 'Rosa Mundi' are over – diascias, for example, would not be tall enough to show above the roses, and would have to be replanted each year after the myosotis were over.

Beyond these long narrow beds four outer beds, edged with 'Hidcote' lavender, are filled to capacity with roses, and between these are spring bulbs, with campanulas, penstemon, foxgloves, nicotianas, Jacob's ladders, hardy geraniums, dianthus, sweet Williams and cistus, all in abundance.

A list of roses might be dull, but among my favourites I saw, in one bed, 'Châpeau de Napoléon', 'Tour de Malakoff', 'Robert le Diable', 'Fantin Latour' (these are all Centifolias), and the moss rose 'Blanche Moreau'. Another bed has the Gallicas: 'Madame Plantier' beside 'Tuscany', 'Hippolyte' with 'Charles de Mills', 'Camaïeux', and the beautiful damask rose 'Ispahan'. The third bed has *R. rugosa* 'Agnes' and *R. r.* 'Alba' with a single-flowered Gallica hybrid, 'Complicata', and the shrub roses 'Belle Poitevine' and 'Pink Grootenhorst'. The fourth bed has *R. rubrifolia* (now called *glauca*) with the Albas 'Céleste', 'Königin von Dánemarck, 'Belle Amour' and 'Félicité Parmentier'.

As you can imagine, the scent is rich, especially so as the yew hedges that surround the garden help to keep it confined.

The four inner beds have lower planting, so when you are standing or sitting by Flora at the central circle you can see over these to the tall roses in the outer beds. These are edged with hyssop and infilled profusely with a lovely mixture of small shrubs interplanted with perennials, keeping the colours to white, blues, mauves and yellows – with a touch of red in the autumn. There are hellebores, euphorbia and erysimum for spring; hypericum, standard honeysuckle and nicotianas for summer; and by autumn the hibiscus and fuchsias are in flower.

The main paths running through this whole part of the garden, the knot and the rose garden, are all grass, edged with bricks, thus eliminating edge-clipping and allowing the lavender and hyssop to spread without damaging the grass.

Xa has invented a special support for her vigorous-growing shrub roses: from the top of a central metal post 2 metres (6 ft) tall eight wires are brought down and attached at ground level about 1 metre (3 ft) from the post. Stems are encouraged first to grow to the top of the post, and are then trained out

*L*ooking across the knot garden towards the rose garden laid out in 1982. The eight square knot beds are designed with clipped box. Those in this picture are filled with herbs which were grown in Tudor times and used in the kitchen as well as the still room. There are three varieties of thyme, hyssop and winter savoury, chives and marjoram, grey and purple sage, lemon balm and rosemary, pineapple mint and spearmint.

Beyond these you can see the long rectangular beds filled with 'Rosa Mundi' and edged with catmint (nepeta). The other rose beds have 'Hidcote' lavender and hyssop as edging. All the roses are underplanted with perennials and low shrubs to keep the ground covered through the year.

and down the wires; flowers will develop all along these stems, so making a complete rose mound, or crinoline. On my visit, bushes of *R*. 'Madame Plantier' and *R*. 'Tuscany Suberb' were a myriad of colour. Other roses Xa recommends for the same treatment are *R*. 'Tour de Malakoff' and *R*. 'Céleste'.

You will notice that, although this is called the 'rose garden', the roses are actually infilled and supplemented by many perennials and biennials. Xa dislikes the look of bare earth – wasted planting space. This also means that in winter, though the roses have bare stems, the ground has a covering of green leaves.

The statue of Flora holding a garland of roses is the important centre-piece between the rose beds. She catches your eye in the distance when you are standing on the bank above the moat, and then as you approach you can see beyond her into the parkland, as a 2-metre-wide (6 ft) section of the yew hedge has been clipped to only 1 metre (3 ft) high. Flora stands on her pedestal within a circle defined with brick, and around this is a brick square and then another brick circle. The soil is covered with golden thyme, reflecting the sun. Bulbs – narcissus, tulips and lilies – add their own seasonal touch. It seems as though Flora has just stepped inside, to pose on her pedestal while the roses are in flower.

The west garden on the other side of the moat which surrounds the house was designed by Dinah, Lady Tollemache in 1965. She made a

*T*he rose garden on the west side of the house was planted by Tim's mother in 1965 with a collection of Hybrid Musk roses. This picture shows them as they are today, growing in beds under the old brick wall. Xa is infilling these to make a great collection. You will recognize 'Penelope', 'Buff Beauty' and others popularized by Gertrude Jekyll and Vita Sackville-West, but some of the later varieties may be new to you: the American 'Bishop Darlington', or 'Hamburg', or 'Erfurt', and the rarely grown 'Daybreak' and 'Thisbe'.

The beds are edged with 'Hidcote' lavender and underplanted with London pride. Planting in the parterre beds is now box and santolina, to replace the original twice-yearly bedding-out.

The fluted stone urn on its pedestal was part of the original design, and is now planted with bulbs and geraniums. The brick pillars are surmounted by the winged horse Pegasus, which is the Tollemache family crest.

parterre garden with the bedding-out changed regularly twice a year. Beyond this, under the brick wall (dating back to 1745) of the old vegetable garden, she planted a collection of the Hybrid Musk roses, so popular then, influenced by Vita Sackville-West: 'Penelope', 'Cornelia', 'Felicia', 'Pax', 'Prosperity', 'Buff Beauty' – all names to entice us. Many of them are still flowering well but Xa has infilled between them with campanulas, peonies, London pride, and more reliable perennials as well as ground-cover plants.

Xa wisely has not altered the layout of the parterre but has eliminated the bedding-out by using a permanent planting of santolina and lavender edged with box, all of which retain their colour throughout the year. This not only involves less work but is, I believe, also more in keeping with the architecture and colour of the red-brick house.

The kitchen garden is full of flowers and fruit. Tim found some old records showing that it was originally divided into eight sections, so they decided to re-create this without making even more work. Off a wide central grass path run lateral paths to form four patches on each side, for vegetables. The main path is lined with generously planted perennial beds backed with climbers trained on horizontal supports. These, in high summer, veil the vegetables growing behind them in the eight squares. Xa and her gardeners have made tunnels over the lateral paths, where sweet peas, gourds and runner beans are planted in spring.

The walls of the kitchen garden, built in 1730, provide a diversity of planting opportunities. In spring the border along the south-facing wall is full of tulips, iris and peonies, with hostas between them and by the beginning of June this border has become mainly foliage.

*T*he brick walls of the kitchen garden were built in 1745, and Tim found old records showing that this garden was originally divided into eight sections. The plan has been re-created, with a wide central grass path off which run lateral paths. The spectacular borders of herbaceous plants are backed with climbing roses trained on wires. Xa is a knowledgeable rose grower and has chosen 'Albertine', 'New Dawn', 'Adélaïde d'Orléans', 'The Garland', 'Bush Rambler', 'Madame Isaac Pereire' and others – all soft colours to blend with the perennials.

On a visit through June to September, you will find a great selection of perennials. Here are dark purple delphiniums, lilies, penstemon, aruncus, salvias, veronicas, asters and huge cardoons. Pastel colouring in early summer gives way later in the year to the stronger yellows and bronze of solidago, heleniums, sunflowers and dahlias, all inviting to the Eagle Gate which leads to the spring border of tulips, iris and peonies.

WOODSIDE

Sometimes ideas come instantly, you may have the perfect solution. This happened on my first visit to Woodside when I was strongly aware that as you stand at the front door you can see through the house into the garden on the further, south-east side. This view must inevitably continue on. A water feature was needed, and an adaptation of the famous fountain canal at the Generalife in Granada, with its arching water jets, would create a continuous vista.

The idea of surrounding the rill with scented borders enclosed by trelliswork came later. It was planned to give fragrance at all times of the year. Also, overlooked from several of the windows of the house, the design must be strong. Wide paths are intended for walking through a garden two or three abreast while talking, socializing, but the essence of a scented garden is narrow curving paths where you expect to stroll, pausing to catch the fragrance of honeysuckles, roses, philadelphus and viburnums as they waft their scent upon the air.

There must be tall features to give permanent height, so there are standards – viburnums, syringas and *Rosa* 'Nozomi'. Planted close by the paths are sarcococca, narcissus, hyacinths and choisya for winter and spring, then when these are over scented summer bedding is added. Each year will have a difference, but the stalwarts – scented-leaved geraniums, heliotrope, lemon verbena and nicotiana – are infilled generously between sage, box and teucrium. A permanent planting with santolina, lavender, violas, pennyroyal and rosemary, together with more roses, all help to keep the borders full with continuing fragrance.

This is where the skill and patience of the gardener is all-important. Dead-headed through the summer and even protected in autumn, these plants will keep on giving of their best until the choisyas and sarcococcas come into flower, often before Christmas. The roses and honeysuckle on the trellis will be giving occasional blooms until the time comes to prune them back, preparing for next year.

The rainbow borders were originally one long, thin, uninspiring border in front of a hawthorn hedge, punctuated by a line of trees which gave unwanted shade and took most of the moisture. It was essential to give this bed more importance, so we widened it and provided a colour scheme. Borders this length (50 metres/55 yd) can be difficult to work through – how do you get to the back without treading on treasures, and what about your wheelbarrow? The solution was to divide it into five sections with grass paths running diagonally between them. The paths are not apparent until you reach them, giving the border a continuous appearance.

All the beds have a framework of shrubs for autumn and winter interest. In the first and the last beds are hot bright colours – red, orange and strong yellows, especially good in autumn. The theme in the beds next to them is pink and white with grey and dark green foliage. The centre bed has

In summer the scented garden keeps its theme. Nicotiana, fragrant pelargoniums, heliotrope, lemon verbena and dianthus fill the beds, planted around the lilacs, standard viburnums and roses.

Water in the garden gives sound and movement. The water spouting on to the narrow canal provides both. Inspired by the arching water jets at the Generalife in Granada, this view is seen as you enter the house, walk through its main rooms and into the scented garden.

Clay pots stand at each jet and are kept full with seasonal flowers. Here blue agapanthus and pink diascias mix with the tumbling flowers of the annual *Specularia speculum*. The way through the pavilion leads around the house and indoor swimming pool to the Roman terrace and the two cottage gardens.

mauves and blues ranging from dark delphiniums to the purple of *Eryngium* × *tripartitum*, whose stems match their spiky flowers.

This bed has definitely been the most difficult to fill with interest through the year. In early spring grape hyacinths and scillas predominate – luckily there are no mauve narcissus! For summer and autumn, agapanthus, blue stokesia, *Penstemon* 'Sour Grapes' and campanulas were planned, and we have used cream and grey to supplement the mauves and blues. *Agastache urticifolia* 'Alba' flowers generously for weeks, and *Nepeta mussinii* (*N.* × *faassenii)* is a good corner plant at the back.

This style of planting, again, needs much skilled upkeep and knowledge of the habit of plants, otherwise it becomes untidy and lacking in finesse when it should be brimming with ordered interest. Helen, who was head gardener when these beds were first planted, kept them under her constant care for three years – now she is married and looks after her baby instead, but I hope the good work will go on.

There will be special days later in the season, when the light is perfect and the hot beds in the rainbow borders will glow with crimson-red *Aster novae-angliae* 'Andenken an Alma Pötschke', and the large leaves of *Bergenia* 'Sunningdale' and the small leaves of *Euonymus alatus* have turned fiery red. *Sedum* 'Autumn Joy' will blend with *Chrysanthemum* 'Mei-kyo', and the red penstemons and diascias will go on flowering until the first frosts. *Verbena* 'Silver Anne' and *V.* 'Sissinghurst' are both almost hardy and will flower under the protection of taller herbaceous plants until late autumn. But while we are enjoying these colours, the routine of bulb planting, of over-wintering the half-hardies, of ordering seeds has to go on. If the plants are not waiting in the wings to take their turn in season, there will be gaps, with bare soil in spring and summer.

*T*he rainbow borders, in all 50 metres (55 yd) long, provided much scope in their original design and planting. Now they must rely on the head gardener to keep them interesting through the year. An established hawthorn hedge provides a good background, and a 90 cm (36 in) path between this and the borders allows access to the back of the beds.

The five borders, which appear continuous, have enough shrubs to give them winter interest, then a generous display of early bulbs and tulips followed by perennials and annuals to infill the gaps when the tulips are over. The edges are kept filled with lamium, helianthemums, sedums, violas. The pink *Lythrum* 'The Rocket' and cream *Agastache urticifolia* 'Alba' provide vertical features among the rounded shapes of verbena and dwarf gypsophila.

WINFIELD HOUSE

*I*t was kind of the American Ambassador to the Court of St James's, Admiral Crowe, to allow me to visit the embassy garden in Regent's Park. You may wonder about the inclusion of a garden in the heart of London, the home of an American, but to me it has the atmosphere of a grand English country garden. Standing on its spacious lawn, you are surrounded by a thick perimeter of trees, and with overflowing flower beds in the English style.

You might well be in the heart of the country, far removed from the bustle of the metropolis.

Furthermore, as I walk around English gardens I am constantly aware of the great debt we owe to America, for the hundreds of plants that have come to us across the Atlantic. They have changed the faces of our gardens, our parks and our woodlands, enriching them with introductions which have now become part of our countryside.

I visited Winfield House for the first time early in June 1995. The sudden change from the urgency of early morning traffic to the calm of the garden at Winfield is dramatic. When the lodge-keeper has opened the handsome but discreet iron gates to allow you inside, pause to pass the time of day with him. He will explain how the dense planting just inside the garden around the road (the Inner Circle of Regent's Park) dulls the sounds of cars, then direct you along the short semicircular drive to the embassy house, with its classical façade redesigned in 1954. He has already told the household of your arrival, and as you approach the portico with its two Tuscan columns the front door opens and you are made welcome.

Pass through the immediate entrance hall into the 12 metre (40 ft) long reception room – the nerve centre of the residence. A portrait of Thomas Jefferson (one of my heroes) hangs on your right, reminding us that this residence is part of the United States of America. There are flowers everywhere, in pots and as floral arrangements, all done by Stephen Crisp, head gardener since 1987. Here the ambassador and his wife greeted me.

What, I wondered, was Ambassador Crowe's greatest enjoyment in his English garden? The answer, fitting from an admiral, came without hesitation. 'I never get tired of looking at the lawns – sort of like watching the ocean.' I was delighted. He can look out of his windows and see this extensive, undulating sea of green, of oceanic proportions, in its different moods. It looks at its best when it has just been mown. 'How much time do you spend on the lawn?' I asked with tongue in cheek, hoping my joke was not too English. 'The gardeners do the mowing, once a week I think.' It was looking immaculate.

I then asked Mrs Crowe what aspect of the garden she loved most. 'I love it all, but especially when we can share it with others.' This immediately warmed me to the charming lady who is the wife of the current United States representative in diplomatic and social circles in England. She reaches

The present-day view from the dining-room windows on the east side of the house. This is the work of Peter Coats, done for Ambassador and Mrs Annenberg (1969–74). The geometric pattern is defined by well-established box edging and infilled with white flowers to reflect the trelliswork. The formal rose garden beyond has 'Iceberg' and 'Ballerina' roses with pillars of climbing *Rosa* 'Golden Showers'.

The statue of Barbara Hutton, the Woolworth heiress, was found later by Ambassador and Mrs Price in the studio of Antonio Berti, the famous Florentine sculptor. She is now a dramatic central feature sitting on a stark white pedestal.

out to many people: children who come to Christmas parties, staff and their families, American citizens who now live and work here; if they feel homesick for the United States, they can 'touch base' with her and immediately feel they have a friend in England.

As I sat talking to the ambassador and his wife, I was conscious of wanting to know more about the history of the place. Later, when walking round the garden with the remarkably able head gardener, Stephen Crisp, he unfolded much of the interesting story.

The land on which the present house was built was once part of a great forest with wooded glades, deer, wild bulls and boars, an ideal hunting-ground for Henry VIII, and a setting for Queen Elizabeth to entertain visiting dignitaries. Charles II had the area 'disparked', but it remained rural until the early nineteenth century, when John Nash began elaborate plans for its development. Only eight of the fifty-six villas he designed were built, and in 1825 Decimus Burton built Hertford Villa – later called St Dunstan's Lodge – on the site of the present-day Winfield House, where the surrounding grounds occupy 4.8 hectacres (12 acres) of Regent's Park (named in honour of the Prince Regent).

In 1936 the Woolworth heiress Barbara Hutton bought the property,

pulled down the Regency house, which was in bad repair, and built a red-brick Georgian-style house in its place. This she named Winfield House, after her maternal grandfather. Barbara lived here until the Second World War broke out in 1939, when she returned to America. During the war, near-misses from German bombs damaged the roof, and damp ruined the parquet floors and spoilt the fine interiors. When Barbara returned to see the house in 1976, she immediately decided to give the whole property to the United States Government, to be repaired and then become the official residence of the American Ambassador to the Court of St James's. And thus it is today.

From this brief history it is clear that the grounds have undergone a varied span of plantings. Oaks are long-lived, and there are other trees which date back to the 1820s when the 3rd Marquess of Hertford lived here in his small twelve-acre park. We can imagine a garden of that time, with a terrace, a well-kept lawn (Budden had recently invented the lawn-mower), and a large conservatory (Nash had already built the fine conservatory at Barnsley Park). There would be seats, planters, urns, serpentine paths, a grand flight of steps with a wrought-iron balustrade. Gardening is partly in the mind, and I was imagining the garden not only as it was in 1825, but also as it looks in other seasons in 1995.

During the years that Barbara Hutton lived here, she planted thousands of trees and shrubs – the hollies were already here, and so were the yew hedges, a feature of the garden today. Someone, sometime, must have done much earth-moving: the ground has a pleasing 'rolling' appearance, with 'knolls' where Stephen has planted a wide variety of shrubs, trees and perennials to achieve year-long interest.

Garden designers often have their own 'signature', and Peter Coats, with his unerring eye for symmetry and design, has left his mark at Winfield House. Ambassador and Mrs Walter Annenberg (1969–74) asked Peter to improve the view from the dining-room windows on the east side of the house. He created an interesting parterre with white-painted trelliswork, to which Stephen has added four large conical boxwoods in Versailles planters. Peter was always clever with his paving patterns; here he made a central circle of cobbles, and used bricks for the main paths. Now there is an appealing statue of Barbara Hutton, made by Antonio Berti and discovered by Ambassador and Mrs Charles Price (1983–89) in Berti's studio in Florence. Peter also designed the formal rose garden, edged with lavender and filled with 'Iceberg' and 'Ballerina' roses, with pillars of climbing *R*. 'Golden Showers'.

From this formal rose garden you walk into the more informal rose garden, designed by Sir Peter Shepherd, a gift from Ambassador and Mrs John Louis of Chicago (1981–83) and Lila Acheson Wallace – the *Reader's Digest* heiress – and known as 'the American contribution to English

Great credit must be given since 1987 to Stephen Crisp, the head gardener, who manages this garden as though it were his own but always referring to his changing American ambassadorial employers. The sun hits down on this south-west-facing border where the soil is very poor and stony, and now filled by Stephen with a few evergreens (including *Magnolia grandiflora* in the foreground) and deciduous trees (sorbus, acers and pyrus) as a background for *Santolina chamaecyparissus*, *Hebe* 'Pewter Dome', cistus and lavender. All the plants are appropriate to their demanding site.

gardens'. Nancy-Mary Goodall helped in the choice of roses for this garden. These are all carefully labelled and include forty-one different old and shrub roses, forty-five Hybrid Teas and Floribundas, and twelve different climbers. The miniature roses planted around the edges were originally used as decoration for a party in the house.

This rose garden now also has a touch of Stephen Crisp's planting. Backing up the roses are plenty of perennials, chosen to be at their best from June until September, even October. The edging is cleverly thought out, with bergenia, nepeta, lavender and santolina. It hides the bare legs of the roses in winter and spring and, maybe more importantly, it prevents birds flicking mulch out on to the lawn and the paths, and on to the York stone paving in the centre around the rose dome. Stephen describes this paved area as giving a sort of breathing space in the heart of the garden.

The underplanting around the roses is worth noticing. There are lovely drifts of peonies for May – their foliage is beautiful as it emerges in spring, and keeps the ground covered through the summer. There are perennials, *Phlox subulata*, heucherella, *Viola labradorica*, *Tolmiea menziesii*, pulmonaria, and in spring cottage-garden tulips are mingled with love-in-a-mist – grown from seed the previous autumn.

Height is all-important in every planting: on each corner in this garden are obelisks, with a climbing rose and *Clematis* × *jackmanii*; Stephen adds sweet peas, for extra interest, scent and colour.

Beyond the rose garden is the secret garden. You pass under a living archway created by old overhanging yews into an enclosed garden, where the emphasis is on architectural plants and well-defined shapes. The predominant colours are white, gold, blues and greys. *Euonymus fortunei* 'Emerald Gaiety' and *E. f.* 'Emerald 'n' Gold' grow with *Choisya ternata* 'Sundance' and golden privet. By June and continuing through the summer the hostas and hesperis (dame's violets), 'Iceberg' roses, delphiniums and tall yellow scabious dominate, with hypericum and cut-leaved sambucus (elder) providing a strong back-up. This secret garden hidden between hedges – the essence of the English garden, in an American setting – is where I imagine Mrs Crowe coming to sit quietly, to relax after a busy day entertaining.

It is important to have different moods in a garden. On my visit the sun was beating down at midday on the broad bank, hot and dry, facing south-west. Stephen's planting here is interesting, so much so that I asked him to draw out his design for me. The structural background planting is of evergreen and deciduous trees – sorbus species, acers, including *A. pseudoplatanus* 'Brilliantissimum', *Magnolia grandiflora* and *Pyrus salicifolia* 'Pendula'. The shrubs are choisya, *Deutzia* × *hybrida* 'Montrose', rosemary, *Cistus* 'Sunset' and *C.* 'Silver Pink', and *Senecio* 'Sunshine'; stark white stems of *Rubus cockburnianus* spring through *Phlomis fruticosa*. At the front is *Helichrysum angustifolium*, with a strong curry scent, and the more discreet *Hebe pagei*, *H.* 'Pewter Dome' and *H. albicans*.

Additional plantings include blue perovskia, sisyrinchium, *Lavatera* 'Ice Cool', the ground-covering *Convolvulus cneorum*, as well as a strongly scented *Lippia citriodora*. The whole bed catches the maximum amount of sunlight during the warmest part of the day.

The day of my visit was extremely hot, so after sitting to admire and absorb the planting on this dry bank, I was ready to walk and then sit in the shady glade. When Stephen arrived as head gardener this area was a real backwater, unloved and neglected – in fact, it was used as a convenient place to keep the gang-mowers and other pieces of equipment: there has to be somewhere to hide such things – but he sensed it was a perfect place for a glade.

Changing moods and themes in a large garden are essential and it is imporant to have corners where a busy owner can sit without disturbance. The wife of the ambassador must find this secret garden restful and satisfying.

Here the predominant colours are soothing – blue, gold, grey and white. A golden broom, *Cytisus × praecox* 'Allgold' grows beside and over a blue-flowered ceanothus. For greys there are drifts of rue, *Senecio* 'Sunshine' and *Helichrysum angustifolium*, with dianthus for scent. As summer progresses, the pink, white and rose-coloured cistus will be in full flower, along with hardy fuchsia, French lavender and *Hebe* 'Autumn Glory' and 'Great Orme'. Euonymus, both the gold- and the silver-leaved forms, make useful edging plants.

Thanks to the trees planted in Barbara Hutton's time there is plenty of shade, providing the ideal situation for understorey plants which need dappled light. Hydrangeas predominate, surrounded by hostas and astilbes. Drifts of aquilegias, hellebores, foxgloves and aruncus grow in the shade of skimmias and rodgersias; the azaleas that give spring colour must not be forgotten. On rainy days the character is green-ness, not gloom, and when the sun beats down it is a wonderful relief to sit here in the cool.

The glade has an atmosphere of calm, accentuated by a seat and an old pear tree. Mrs Crowe confided that she and her husband go there occasionally to sit, and talk quietly together. 'People ask us if we're going to the country for the weekend. I say we're already in the country, we don't need to go anywhere else.'

BLEDLOW MANOR

The mellow red-brick Manor House at Bledlow in Buckinghamshire has been in the Carrington family for nearly two hundred years, but the garden is young in comparison. I believe it is now one of the most interesting twentieth-century English country gardens.

When Lord and Lady Carrington decided to make this their home, it was a typical farmhouse surrounded by old barns, cattle yards and fields. Peter, with his love of trees, soon planted beech and oak – hardwoods, for posterity – between the front gate and the house. Fifty years on, these are mature and stand in a well-kept lawn, giving the entrance a peaceful and dignified atmosphere, in winter as well as in summer. It does not need flowers, they would detract from the glory of the trees.

In 1966 a cataclysmic event occurred: the fifteenth-century tithe barn close to the south side of the house burnt down. This was the moment for change. Iona, wanting more flower borders, and Peter, always enjoying new projects, decided to invite Robert Adams, a young designer, to draw up plans for a garden to encompass the house. They were delighted by his imaginative ideas, and a firm and lasting rapport was established.

Today the garden has Robert Adams's formal structure enhanced by Iona's flower borders and Peter's imagination and humour. This is another garden where there have always been two master-hands at work. Iona has a great love of flowers – she wakes in the middle of the night and thinks up the various plant combinations she would love to have. Peter admits that he does not like standing still, preferring always to have some new enterprise in hand.

Gardens must have their serious side – good structure, solid planting, summer scents – but a garden without humour lacks an important quality. The Manor House has all of these. To me the humour comes through very forcibly – especially in Peter's sculpture garden, with its gorilla and two tumbling figures, and Iona's honest statement that 'Peter wakes up in the middle of the night and thinks of shapes. Luckily he sleeps very well – otherwise we'd have even more shapes in the garden.'

There is much more to see than only vegetables in the potager at Bledlow Manor. Peter Carrington's eight-pillar bandstand covered with climbing roses is the central feature from which four stone paths radiate and emerge. On each side, beds are filled with reliable perennials – peonies, tall strong blue delphiniums, aquilegias, astrantias and tall onopordums. They give a luxuriant feeling in summer, and are a foretaste of the English country garden planting which awaits visitors as they walk around the garden.

Behind these are carefully pruned apples on dwarfing stock – 'Greensleeves', 'Sunset' and 'Red Ellison'.

The success of this garden is the seemingly effortless way in which it has become their private hobby, to which they both turn from their public life. I am increasingly aware how important gardens are to their owners; they can walk in them and discover a peace which has been lost in the late twentieth century. My wise mother put it this way: 'Remember that your brain and body are like a grandfather clock that regularly needs to be wound up to maintain its vigour.' We all do this in different ways: by rest, or by complete change, or by becoming absorbed in a hobby which satisfies our creativity – such as gardening.

On the south side of the house, where the old tithe barn burnt down, there is now a formal enclosed garden. A gravel path is lined with standard *Viburnum carlesii*, chosen by Iona for their intoxicating scent in April. Now forty years old, they have huge mop heads, but two are dying. Iona and the head gardener Frank Bailey are having a difficult time finding suitably large replacements.

The gravel path leads you down steps through an opening in a beech hedge to a sunk garden with a brick-edged pond. Beyond is a brick granary

*O*ne of the series of architectural gardens designed by Robert Adams for the Carringtons leads from the rose garden into the St Peter garden. Once he stood on the north-west corner of the Houses of Parliament; then, his hands and toes eroded with age, he was brought by Peter Carrington to Bledlow.

This garden is like a paintbox, each wedge-shaped, box-edged bed has its own colour – white variegated *Iris pallida*, lavender, santolina and *Festuca glauca*. Surrounded by tall yew hedges, the pathway curves and leads you round into the garden where the armillary sphere is the centrepiece in an all-green garden paved with brick and gravel.

Leading from the strong architectural gardens to the north side of the house, Iona has in-filled Robert Adams' designs with her own planting. Brick paths surround the raised beds and lavender frames and scents the picture. The beds are filled with one of Iona's favourite roses, *R*. 'English Rose', and *R*. 'English Garden'. The pastel tones give way to stronger colours in the perennial borders beyond. The brick piers with their stone balls lead you across a lane towards the statue garden, and the trees are an essential background to this whole scene.

– one of the remaining old farm buildings, dating from 1725 – and beside this is a new white-weather-boarded, hipped-roof gazebo, influenced by the pair at the end of the red borders at Hidcote. Here Peter displays some of the collection of presents given to him on his visits around the world as Foreign Secretary – a rather weird assortment. This garden is carefully aligned to be enjoyed from the sitting-room window; it is also the garden into which visitors arrive on open days for the National Gardens Scheme.

We must not dally: there is a great deal to see. Peter will take you into his vegetable garden, where there is much more than just vegetables. On the way to the central 'bandstand' covered with climbing roses are carefully pruned apples – 'Greensleeves', 'Sunset', 'Red Ellison' – on dwarfing rootstock, trained into balls over wire hoops. On one axis these trees are underplanted with useful herbs, on the other with perennials, mainly delphiniums and peonies.

Frank Bailey has worked here since 1987, and loves the vegetable garden most of all. Talking with Frank reassured me of the importance of continuity in the garden – he knows where the first frost will fall, where the beans and brassicas will do best. Such practical knowledge and experience are vital, and so is tidiness.

From the potager we moved on into the games area, a swimming pool and croquet lawn. We discussed family croquet, and Peter admitted with a twinkle that when they have visitors, 'We always win – we have our own rules.' I espied a robust climber on the poolhouse wall which surprised me, a *Dregea sinensis*, which does not survive with us in the Cotswolds. It has been at Bledlow for a decade and now produces fruit.

At the foot of the sloping lawn on the north side of the manor and running parallel to Iona's herbaceous borders is an ornamental pool designed by Robert Adams, long and narrow and edged all round with brick. Here I joined Iona for a chat.

Iona has a special love for her perennials and half-hardies. She likes soft colours, scented flowers and aromatic leaves. She plans mainly on paper, and is determined to have good colour combinations, using cream, grey, yellows and blues, and to extend the flowering time in the borders into September and October. We discussed red borders, and agreed that they are difficult to achieve successfully – and anyway do we enjoy them? I was surprised that there were no tulips in spring, but Iona explained that she had given up growing them except in tubs: in the borders, muntjacks from a nearby hill wait until they are in bud, then come down and simply take the heads off, leaving bare stalks.

Iona's choice of plants for her herbaceous borders is sophisticated, and includes many that are unusual. There are groups of *Morina longifolia* with thistle-like leaves and whorls of pinky-white flowers on half-metre (18 in) stems, narrow-leaved *Asphodeline lutea*, eremurus and both the white and the purple dictamnus. In the back of the border are *Artemisia lactiflora* 'Quizhou' and *Lysimachia ephemera*, to flower amongst the asters in September. I so agree with Iona that it is easier to learn about brilliant plants (and you must always be selective!) by visiting gardens and taking notes than it is by reading. She finds that Christopher Lloyd's writing is always an inspiration to her.

It is important to have names for the different parts of your garden, so you can explain to your gardener where you want him to work and to your friends where they will find you. At Bledlow the first of the three architectural spaces, all of which are hedged with yew, is called the rose garden. It has kept its name even though most of the roses have been taken out, or changed. Peter disliked the originals and Iona chose others to fill the central beds – 'Iceberg' and 'Korresia', roses she could pick for the house. The outer borders are filled with well-shaped, predominantly grey-leaved shrubs, all well developed and many of them evergreen, and the planting is repeated, giving a consistent look. There are *Brachyglottis* 'Sunshine' (Iona and I still call this *Senecio*), large mounds of *Viburnum davidii*, lavender,

*I*ona's perennial border is firmly edged with brick paving. I like the way in which the edge is so well filled with *Stachys lanata* – alliums are an inspired idea to plant among them – and euphorbia, iris, sedums, bergenias and aquilegias make a continuous edging. This border is a summer wonder and should be captured at its peak for colour and scent. The height of the eremurus takes your eyes effortlessly upwards to the trees beyond.

rosemary, choisya and *Lotus hirsutus*, better known as *Dorycnium*. A brick path surrounds the central rose beds and then invites you under an archway in the yew into the second of these architectural rooms – the St Peter garden.

A well-weathered statue of the apostle looks after this little garden. He used to hang on the north-west corner of the Houses of Parliament – then when his hands and toes became eroded he was sold, and came to Bledlow. I love the moss on his head. This garden curves, and the wedge-shaped beds make a neat geometrical pattern. They are edged with box and filled with blocks of colour, rather like a huge paintbox: there is *Santolina chamaecyparissus*, *Festuca glauca*, white-variegated *Iris pallida*, and lavender.

The brick path continues, and takes you into the last compartment, the most architectural of the three. Here an armillary sphere is the centre-piece, almost enclosed by four matching box sculptures. Solid cubes are topped

*T*he long pool is divided into four by brick walkways. Water-lilies of different colours cover the surface, and with the lawn it creates a serene scene. There is a seat at one end to sit quietly and see the perennial border, so carefully planned by Iona to look luxuriant from May through to autumn.

Here delphiniums, foxtail lilies and young kniphofias send up spikes between a hardy geranium, peonies and rounded foliage shapes. Look at this bed from either end and notice its inspired planting.

by impressive balls, echoing the shape of the metal globe. This is an all-green garden, paved with bricks and gravel.

The Lyde Garden, over the road from the Manor House, is an inspiration at all times of the year, but I love it best in April when leaf buds are swelling and there is still a transparent look between the trees and bushes. I must explain that this garden is in a deep ravine created by springs which eventually reach the River Thames via the small River Lyde. The ravine is dramatic, with Bledlow church poised precipitously above.

Elm disease struck in the early 1970s, and with more light a wilderness of brambles, nettles and ash saplings sprang up. The prospect was daunting – the Carringtons could either leave it to nature, or plan. As both Peter and Iona are do-ers, once again Robert Adams was called in. The first thing to be done was to clear the mess and channel the spring-water into a series of small ponds. Peter and Iona found this a trying time: 'Neighbours thought we were creating a place for the local cement works, and that we were ruining an attractive wildlife area.' How wrong they were.

The east side was the drier, and here on the steep slope they put in *Sorbaria kirilowii arborea* (a lovely name for a beautiful plant that flowers briefly in August) and also euonymus (spindles), colutea and corylus. As Peter explained, *Prunus lusitanica* and *P. laurocerasus* supply the form, and philadelphus the scent. Geraniums, vincas and symphytums have spread and now mask the paths. A seedling *Ailanthus altissima* has put on a metre (3 ft) a year – and to the Carrington's astonishment, everything has grown.

This was all on the dry side of the ravine, and they were so encouraged by the progress that they decided to tackle the damp western side. Robert Adams again came to the rescue, designing a rustic wooden bridge and pathway with steps to cross over the damp area, so that it is possible to walk this side keeping your feet dry. You can hear the sound of the water as it falls down the side of the ravine, feeding the three pools even in times of drought.

The really marshy places have gunneras, ferns, astilbes, hostas, primulas growing in profusion. Higher on the slope willows, *Cornus alba* 'Elegantissima' and aralia are planted. We all know that the weeping willow, *Salix babylonica* 'Pendula', will do well if its roots are in a damp place; so will the swamp cypress, *Taxodium distichum* – and now there is the prehistoric tree from China, *Metasequoia glyptostroboides*, for our gardens. Peter and Iona have planted all these as well as two golden poplars.

Iona admits that the Lyde Garden needs much less time to keep in order than her perennial borders. Now it is in perfect shape, and I know that they will have to stay on top of the pruning or the shrubs and trees will get on top of them. The Lyde Garden is open to anyone, any time of the year. How lucky for the inhabitants of Bledlow, knowing they can walk here whenever they wish. It is their garden as well as the Carringtons'.

THE GROVE

ady Pamela and Mr David Hicks moved into the nineteenth-century farmhouse and property at The Grove, Brightwell Baldwin in south Oxfordshire in 1980, and over sixteen years the garden around the house has matured, with hedges and pleached trees grown to their ultimate chosen height. Looking out from the garden into the surrounding flat farmland, there are long avenues, young plantations, and new vistas in three directions.

David Hicks, who made his first complete garden in Suffolk when he was twenty-six, is now a well-known international interior and garden designer, with his own distinctive style. He likes straight lines and symmetry, abhorring 'intestinal' designs; green should dominate around his house – flower beds are kept in a secret, enclosed garden not seen from the house. Here he grows flowers and foliage to be used for cutting for the house.

In David's garden for all seasons, the strong architectural lines and the scale of the ten formal rooms and vistas are apparent throughout the year. In most English gardens the structure becomes less important and defined in summer, overwhelmed by the exuberance of growth and colour: at The Grove, the firm lines of the garden remain dominant – but the walls of the garden rooms have changed from the tawny brown of winter hornbeam and beech leaves and chestnut tracery to a summer green. In winter they are almost transparent (so you catch glimpses within), but in summer they become solid, and you must walk into each garden room to discover its proportions and charm – an early nineteenth-century statue of the discus thrower and two Lutyens seats in one, a collection of magnolias in another. These include 'Edith Bogne', 'Saint George', 'Gallissonière', and 'Nantensis'.

Exploring further, you find the 'red room'. This, a more recent idea, is a space you walk into, to pause rather than sit here. The four walls are copper beech stilt trees underplanted with a copper beech hedge. The

he two-storey pavilion was designed by David Hicks and given to him by Lady Pamela for his sixtieth birthday. The well-proportioned round-topped gate leads from the main garden into the secret garden, where David grows a collection of flowers and foliage to pick for the house. Roses predominate in June and July, but they are intermingled with annuals and perennials from spring through to autumn. The tree peonies are important for their exotic flowers in May, and in June the perennial peonies are ready to pick before the main explosion of roses.

David grows his favourtie nicotianas, *N.* 'Lime Green', *N. sylvestris* and *N. langsdorffii*. Poppies, feverfew, foxgloves and mignonette seed amongst the roses. There are eremurus and *Eucomis bicolor* and lilies in pots all ready to drop into the borders or take into the house. The fragrant *Passiflora alata* grows on the south-facing wall.

The steps from the pavilion lead down into the tiled loggia.

limestone urn in an alcove of beech is set against a stone wall, and a gentle flow of water falls from its brim into a shallow pool at its base. For structure, always necessary in David's plans, four wooden obelisks each have the climbing red rose 'Danse du Feu' billowing through them.

The nearby 'green room' is full of ideas. Two walls are stilt hornbeams with a hornbeam hedge behind. On one side is a collection of boxwood topiary, *Buxus sempervirens*, in square wooden cases made by Peter Church, a trained carpenter as well as one of David's gardeners. These have no bases, so the topiary can root through into the ground. On the other side of the grass path a tailored arrangement of globe artichokes is planted in round plastic terracotta-style pots standing neatly in two straight lines. The plants emerge from a rectangular platform of hawthorn clipped to the height of the pots, the grey artichoke leaves looking handsome all through summer. David has experimented with growing mulberries in another twelve pots, but they proved unsatisfactory with their roots confined so they will be planted out elsewhere in the garden. Figs are potted nearby. They are excellent in pots and with their roots confined will produce a harvest of fruit. At the top of this green garden is a seat flanked on each side by 3.6 metre (12 ft) pylon shapes with *Vitis coignetiae* growing up and through them.

Going back to the see-through wooden fence at the top of the mown lawn, you get a striking view of the two-storey pavilion designed by David and given to him by his wife for his sixtieth birthday. It is an important feature from several viewpoints in the garden. You arrive there along a corridor with hornbeams on your right and a brick wall on your left, then in front of you is a wooden bridge over a narrow canal. David, ever inventive, has a whimsy plan that the bridge will be lowered electrically, like a drawbridge, as he approaches with his guests, and they will cross over and enter the pavilion. This has furniture designed by him and used in his work. From the floor above you can look down on several of the garden rooms, seeing them with a bird's eye view – a place to sit, think, write, draw, without interruption from callers or the telephone.

Also over the bridge is the gate into the secret garden, where he grows flowers to pick for the house. It is a long rectangle with square beds each side and divided by a central path. Here are roses, especially selected by David from the great rose growers David Austin and Peter Beales. Roses on their own can be wonderful for most of the summer, but he takes the opportunity to grow annuals and perennials between them, to fill the beds and cover the soil. Some will emerge before the roses are in flower, others will complement them, and the rest will open later. He uses white stocks, poppies, feverfew, mignonette and foxgloves.

There are also tree peonies, important for their exotic flowers in May, and in June perennial ones are ready to pick just before the main explosion of roses. In autumn their leaves are invaluable as they turn deep red-crimson

In a corner of the secret rose garden (see page 87), David has a novel way of growing his shrub peonies. The pots stand surrounded by box (*Buxus sempervirens* 'Suffruticosa') clipped into squares, each 30 cm (1 ft) high and neatly edged with bricks and gravel. A saddle-stone stands in the centre, creating a satisfying quincunx. The design is a geometry of circles contained in squares.

Notice the wooden grille on the left, the front of a container to house the hosepipe. The climbing roses on the brick wall are 'New Dawn' and 'Rambling Rector'.

$\mathscr{A}$ limestone urn is the centrepiece of David's red garden. Water brims slowly over the top lip and dribbles quietly down the curved sides on to a flat stone, then splashes into the shallow pool below. The red roses 'Danse de Feu' grow through wooden obelisks which can be seen on page 158. The hedges are copper beech,

following David's idea of using standard trees underplanted with hedges of the same species.

The chairs, made by my son Charles, were designed by David for a garden he created at Chelsea in 1984.

and tawny brown streaked with green, making a perfect background foil for autumn flowers.

Hosta leaves will need to be protected all through the year or slugs will spoil them. Slugs, I believe, mate and produce their young in summer, so we have always put out slug pellets (those harmless to cats, dogs and birds) in August; but some live under the soil and eat into the leaves when they are still below ground, so we must try to keep vigilant from March all through summer.

Were I a slug I would remain below ground until after all threat of spring frosts, except when warm days tempted me above ground to devour a fresh salad of all sorts of emerging leaves. The old writers advocate that you surround your most precious plants, tender lettuces and seedlings with prickly holly leaves, or with cinders. David Hicks grows hostas in pots, which prevents slug damage and many plants good for cutting are not prey to slugs. The dramatic leaves of bergenia are important, and so are nepeta and wall germander.

David Hicks has a regular supply of the hardy biennial *Salvia turkestanica*, as a back-up for his roses, but their pungent smell makes it difficult to use them indoors. There are different approaches to annuals and biennials. At Barnsley we scatter poppy seeds almost everywhere, at any time. They are biennials and can be very easily 'weeded out', but where they are allowed to develop they make a great statement through summer and late autumn, and their seed heads are invaluable in dried arrangements.

The different nicotiana look good amongst the roses, and all last well in water. David's favourites are *N.* 'Lime Green', *N. sylvestris* and *N. langsdorffii* which are planted in thick groups allowing some to be picked and others left. Foxgloves make more vertical features, and the *Digitalis purpurea* 'Glittering Surprises' group includes a variety of colours to match and contrast with the roses.

Other useful verticals are the dramatic eremurus, which look wonderful in an indoor arrangment, if you can bear to pick them. Climbing nasturtiums in mixed colours are allowed to wander through the borders, their bright flowers used to decorate summer salads. Roses and lilies are perfect companions, and lots of lilies are planted in pots so they can either be brought indoors to scent the house or dropped into spaces in the rose borders as they come into flower.

Like all of us, David's ideas change, as he becomes more selective, and new things are offered in seed catalogues.

Walking in this garden at The Grove we must watch closely for detail, but it is also important to look up and over into the landscape, for this is the backdrop, with its mature deciduous trees – oaks, limes, beech.

BENINGTON LORDSHIP

Since Saxon times, when Benington Lordship was the site of a large palace and a wooden church, the property has had more than its share of blessings and misfortunes. Through the centuries its owners have been men at the heart of politics and society; but their residences have not always fared so well.

Today the outer and inner baileys, the moat and the ruined keep stand as testament to the splendour of the ancient castle, demolished on the orders of Henry II in the twelfth century. The manor house for several generations of landowners, nearby Benington Park, burnt down, and the Lords of the manor moved into Benington Lordship, an early Georgian house built on the site of the ruined castle and a later, demolished farmhouse. Arthur and Lilian Bott bought the property in 1906, and their grandson Harry inherited the house from his father in 1970.

In the early nineteenth century the owner George Proctor made architectural additions to the house and garden. His idea of creating a summer-house in the ruined curtain wall reveals him to have been a man of sensitivity, while his mock-Norman gatehouse shows that he was not afraid to make a bold statement. It would be interesting to be able to talk to him about his ideas. James Pulham, inventor of the famous Pulhamite stone, was involved in the building of the gatehouse and folly. We can only admire his use of Norman devices, and his own technique.

In this century Harry's grandparents made their mark, creating the garden but spoiling the Georgian symmetry of the house by adding a wing and a veranda on the west side. They had recently returned from a financially successful time in India, and I can imagine them sitting on their new veranda, sipping their sundowners and enjoying the sweeping lawn overlooking a spectacular view. Originally the drive came past the church and along the west side of the house, passing in front of the veranda, so they moved it to its present position: the approach now cuts through the park on the east side. Seventy years later, Sarah Bott has developed the drama of this view with great effect, incorporating two ancient fishponds into the garden, uniting it with the park and creating an interesting winter walk.

When Lilian and Arthur arrived there was a nine-hole golf course in the park; they must have recoiled, read William Robinson, and set about making a typical Edwardian country-house garden with shrubberies, bedding-out, and a walled kitchen garden where enough vegetables could be grown to feed the huge staff considered essential in those times.

Today, Sarah's attitude is remarkably relaxed. She loves the garden and spends much of her time working in it, but does not allow it to dominate her life; she has other interests, her horses, family, and sailing. Brought up by garden-loving parents in Cornwall, she is keenly interested and absorbed in introducing new or unusual varieties.

The garden is kept to a high standard, and in order to do this enough

The rockery designed by Harry Bott's uncle when on leave from the First World War is planned around the spring in the 'top pool'. When the bulbs have died back there are primulas and small shrubs and later, in early summer, euphorbias and diascias. The reflection in summer mirrors texture and shape, and in spring and winter it is the coloured stems of dogwoods and willows which are repeated.

From here you walk up between the herbaceous borders towards the walled kitchen garden.

income must be generated by opening charges and plant sales to finance the wages of the gardening staff – a situation which has arisen in many large established gardens.

Benington Lordship is well known for its spectacular drifts of snowdrops, and rightly so, but Sarah has made it a garden for all seasons. Summer is dominated by roses, old and modern, and by the long herbaceous borders. The rose garden on the south side of the house was laid out by Lilian Bott soon after she and Arthur had completed the addition to the house. Sarah has reduced the number of beds; those in the middle have been grassed over, to save work and overcome rose sickness. New roses have been chosen for their scent and their repeat-flowering qualities. 'Margaret Merril', creamy-white overlaid with a satin-pink sheen, has an exceptional fragrance and – very important – disease-resistant foliage. The warm rose-pink 'Radox Bouquet', a floribunda (60–100 cm/2–3 ft), is good for cutting and highly fragrant, but still only supplied by a few nurseries. These roses are surrounded and interplanted with dwarf iris and aquilegias.

The rose theme continues nearby with a collection of early flowering shrub roses. Among Sarah's favourites is the Rugosa 'Agnes', a rich yellow and amber with a delicious scent, and disease free; it also gives a second crop in late summer. 'Frühlingsduft' – preferred by Sarah to 'Frühlingsgold' – has a scent which wafts on the air, competing, especially on damp days, with the aromatic fragrance of *R. primula*, the Incense Rose, with fern-like leaves.

Visitors are inevitably drawn to the view over the parkland on the west so they go down the wide stone steps, but there is much more to explore before we allow ourselves time to relax on the veranda. A large urn, discovered in the moat, has become a focal point, surrounded by a camomile lawn and *Rosa moyesii* 'Geranium', spectacular in autumn with its vibrant red hips.

On a June day it is best to keep to the area around the house, to give yourself time to appreciate all Sarah's summer planting. Browse through a small sunk garden, once part of the moat, where the central feature is a lead statue of Pantaloon, the Venetian merchant from the harlequinade. He came from Lilian Bott's home in Buckinghamshire, and is surrounded by a succession of summer flowers, white honesty, *Clematis* 'Nelly Moser', white iris, Rose 'Iceberg' and *Lilium auratum*. Continuing this white theme, the *pièce de résistance* is a group of the special white *Agapanthus arboroseus* Ardernei hybrids. I am sure that Sarah must have brought these with her from Cornwall.

Sometimes it is stimulating to keep back a trump card, then produce it as a superb surprise. Hidden away, to be encountered when you are least expecting them, are the twin herbaceous borders, sited so you can approach them from either direction. Looking up the stepped gravel path you have

Sarah's herbaceous borders, divided by a gravel path, run from east to west and are on sloping ground. In this picture you are looking uphill towards the east.

The left-hand border is backed by a 2.5 metre (8 ft) stone wall, and the right-hand border is protected by shrubs. The plants are allowed to luxuriate on to the path, providing satisfactory soft lines. Visitors love the profusion of flowers; many, like aquilegias, honesty and salvias, self-seed. The skill in designing a border this length is combining shapes – rounds with spikes – colours which blend, and every square inch covered in summer.

The evening sun highlights the shapes and colours as you walk up the slope, as in this picture. In the morning as you stand at the top you have the sun behind you, giving a different impression.

a truly dramatic view which Sarah has transformed. She says they are at their best in May and June and later in September and October.

One of the borders, spilling on to the path, is backed by a wall, the other by trees and mixed shrubs, giving an informal background of evergreen trees interspersed with lilacs and early flowering roses, 'Canary Bird', 'Frühlingsgold' and 'Sarah van Fleet', underplanted with white tulips. In May there is a profusion of self-sown white-flowered honesty and aquilegias, of *Smilacina racemosa*, more unusual than Solomon's seal, and of *Alchemilla mollis* leaves, catching the dew.

Herbaceous borders, Sarah will tell you, are not for those who find gardening a necessity rather than a pleasure; they are for people who are prepared to drop in pots of lilies and add trays of seedling snapdragons and asters to a bare space. It is possible to provide a continuous succession of colour in all borders if, like Sarah, you visit other people's gardens, take notes, and then order plants, remembering all the time that every space in your own border must be filled, from April until autumn. In time, by osmosis, choosing a succession of plants to give borders continuous colour and interest will become instinctive.

In her borders Sarah has used lots of penstemon, tradescantias, shaggy annual asters (from seed), polygonums, veronicas, my favourite *Lysimachia ephemerum*, and of course clematis, crocosmia, eupatoriums, monkshoods and Michaelmas daisies.

The excitement of gardening is that each year sees changes, some by the hand of nature and others by the gardener's spirit of adventure.

FOLLY FARM

On a warm sunny summer's morning Emily Lucy Astor and I started our walk round the garden from the front door of the old farmhouse, which leads into the two barn courts. Here is a feeling of an enclosed cottage garden. What first struck me were the two straight paths, unmistakably designed by Sir Edwin Lutyens, with narrow bricks laid in a herringbone pattern and edged with cut stone.

Many of the plants here are evergreen and scented: magnolia, sarcococca, choisya and jasmine. The *polyantha* rose 'Natalie Nypels', introduced into England in 1919, grows in the first 'court' under the house wall; it has a medium-pink flower and blooms continuously through summer. There are ferns, euphorbia and begonia, and clumps of *Helleborus orientalis*. In contrast against the black wall of the barn is a line of the climbing rose 'Iceberg', with *Nepeta mussinii* (described by Gertrude Jekyll as 'a plant that can hardly be overpraised') as an edging and *N.* 'Six Hills Giant' growing strongly behind, in summer hiding any bare stems on the roses.

The focal point at the end of the second path is an urn on a plinth. This is surrounded by four beds of *Rosa* 'Gruss an Aachen', introduced in 1909, a novelty when it was chosen by Gertrude Jekyll for this then newly formed court garden. 'Gruss an Aachen' has deeply cupped flowers filled with many small pearly-pink petals, which fade to a creamy white.

Pause to admire the simple but effective structure here, before you turn right to pass under an archway in the brickwork which brings you in to Lutyens' entrance court. On your right is the front door, one of his additions of 1906. This court, square and formal, originally had four small square lawns intersected by the herringbone paths and edged with box. Now stone paving has been laid to replace the lawn – to reduce work – but the box edging and the bay trees remain. These and the hardy fuchsia are all favourite plants used by Gertrude Jekyll in her plans.

Also characteristic of a Lutyens garden are the enticing seats. Emi-Lu and I had reached the terrace, enclosed on three sides by house walls, and here Hugh Astor was waiting for us. I was longing to hear more about their achievements in the garden since 1951, and their opinion as to how strictly a Gertrude Jekyll planting should be followed.

From where we were sitting we had a perfect, symmetrical view along the impressive canal, part of the original 1906 design. The canal is stone-edged, and the strips of lawn at the far end on each side were originally flower borders, predominantly filled with iris. As Hugh said: 'At this time of the year, with the water-lilies, it looks rather attractive.' I thought of Russell Page's statement that every new plant should be an addition, not a distraction – the iris might have been a distraction from the reflection and the water-lilies.

The canal ends in a mock bridge, built in a mixture of stone and brick, and a balustrade flanked by two flights of well-designed, bull-nosed steps

This canal garden has been likened to the Dutch garden at Westbury Court (1700) and that at Frampton Court in Gloucestershire. This reinforces my belief that there is little new in garden design. The twentieth-century garden designer Russell Page told us that water in the garden has three attributes: reflection, sound and movement. Here is reflection. This is Sir Edwin Lutyens' boldest water canal, typifying his concept of strong lines radiating from the house.

Gertrude Jekyll's design had iris borders along both sides. These have been replaced by lawn for economy of labour, but the simplicity now emphasizes the geometry of the canal. The steps set at right angles are a signature of Lutyens' design work.

leading to a higher level. The architecture is softened by the vigorous summer-flowering climbing rambler, *Rosa* 'The Garland'. Hugh explained that they had planted it as a tribute to Gertrude Jekyll: it was one of her favourite roses – described by her as 'warm white'. It has one spectacular display and is highly scented, but sadly is not repeat-flowering.

Today there is much discussion and controversy about the principles of garden restoration. Should planting be historically correct, or can new plants be added, as surely the owner and designer would have done today? This is a pertinent question at Folly Farm. Hugh explained that they have had to simplify the garden, and also that they have used more modern plants than were available to Gertrude Jekyll: 'I do feel it's a living thing and has to change with the time and the wishes of the owners. Surely a garden shouldn't be fossilized?'

We discussed the labour force, then and now. In the early years fourteen gardeners were employed, and during the 1920s and 1930s there were eight gardeners to maintain the kitchen garden and the pleasure grounds; now Mr Honour and Mr Tate keep up the garden to a constantly high standard. So how is this done? Mechanization helps – lawn mowers and hedge clippers – and bringing in extra labour when needed. Bedding-out is kept to a minimum. The iris borders by the canal have gone, and others – in the parterre garden – are reduced in size. The walled kitchen garden, almost an acre in extent, which provided daily vegetables for the family and their many guests – as well as the indoor staff – required many man-hours of work. Now it has been put down to grass, and it is the flock of Jacob's sheep that does the work.

The proportions of the canal are perfect, a happy example of architect and garden designer working together. Hugh described how the water attracts wildlife: 'We get regular visits from the heron, who is interested in the goldfish, and yesterday there was a kingfisher inspecting the smaller fish – he only takes the tiddlers.' For something like twenty years, spotted fly-catchers have nested on the house wall at the back of the terrace where we were sitting. Birds are creatures of habit, often returning to the place they were hatched, so it is wise to watch out for their nests and protect the fledgling birds from cats.

Lutyens, in his design for the garden, made the best use of the natural change of level. From the terrace where we had been sitting, steps with urns each side lead down to the tank garden and the flower parterre. The tank fits neatly between two wings of the house, and the dark water reflects the strong, slanting buttresses supporting the long low roof. Here there is another sitting place, covered by the roof and with a view over the tank; Emi-Lu says, 'Whenever it's warm enough we sit here and have a meal, that's the great joy.' The planting in the long narrow bed just beyond is the subject of some discussion. In summer it is bedded out with bright pink

*T*he rose garden is a masterpiece of Lutyens' design. Surrounded on all sides by immaculately clipped yew hedges, it is a perfect sanctuary at any time of the year. In summer the scent of roses and lavender pervades.

The planting of roses includes 'Silver Jubilee', scarlet-red 'Lilli Marlene', 'Peace', 'Congratulations', 'Pink Favourite' and 'Korresia'. Height, an all-important feature, is achieved with the standard rose 'The Fairy' and the *Pyrus salicifolia* 'Pendula' on each corner.

geraniums, on which Mr Honour prides himself; he enjoys overwintering them, and taking cuttings – but should this bed have a permanent planting, or does the constant summer colour justify the time and work involved?

Beside the tank garden the planting in the parterre beds has the same quality and character as in Gertrude Jekyll's time, but again the plan has been simplified to reduce labour. Wider grass paths and narrower beds take considerably less maintenance, but this change in no way detracts from the symmetry. The borders used to go right up to the yew hedge, and the roses and buddlejas were then the background plants: these have now been brought forward to make a tall feature along the centre of each border, with a solid planting of perennials on both sides. Now that there are grass paths between the yews and the borders, these have become 'island beds'.

There is a rhythm of roses growing through wooden frames made by Mr Honour – 'Penelope', 'Felicia', and 'Cérise Bouquet', whose arching sprays need support. The planting of perennials is carefully thought out, both in colour and design. Deep purple *Salvia nemorosa* 'East Friesland' and hardy geraniums complement the delphiniums, lupins and day lilies, all softened by grey *Stachys byzantina*, gypsophila, *Malva* 'Rose Queen' and *Campanula lactiflora*. There are penstemon for July, August and September, among white lilies and phlox.

This garden is bisected by a wide Lutyens-designed stone path, and in the centre a Purbeck stone basin serves as a bird bath. After consultation between Mr Honour and Vernon Russell-Smith more herbaceous borders have been grassed over in the parterre garden, where the axis of the central stone path leads through the yew hedge. The axis is now an impressive avenue of crab apples, *Malus* × *zumi* 'Golden Hornet' alternating with *M. coronaria* 'Charlottae'. In spring these have pale pink blossom, in summer they give welcome shade, and in autumn a fine crop of fruit. At whatever season you visit Folly Farm, there is always interest.

July is the prime time to enjoy the rose garden. This is a sunken, square garden, surrounded by yew hedges, part of the original planting. Gertrude Jekyll wrote in *Roses for English Gardens*:

> We are growing impatient with the usual Rose garden, generally a
> sort of target of concentric rings of beds placed upon turf, often with
> no special aim at connected design with the portions of the garden
> immediately about it, and filled with plants without a thought of their
> colour effect or any other worthy intention.

This garden has dignity as well as mystery. As you come upon it from a corner of the parterre garden, you should pause at the top of the stone steps and view the shapes and the planting. For a moment I imagined I was talking to Edwin Lutyens, thinking through with him this successful design. He had a passion for geometry, and as an architect he had studied Serlio and Palladio and come to realize the vital importance of marrying the garden with the house. Paths, like passages, are an essential part of the structure but sometimes, as in this rose garden, the eye can be deceived. Lutyens was a master at this. Then I realized it was Hugh Astor who was saying, 'What looks like a semicircle [referring to the steps] is in fact not quite a semicircle, and what looks like a straight edge is, in fact, slightly curved.'

In the central feature, where a raised bed is surrounded by water, the lavender is in flower; the lilies will have come through earlier. While we are sitting on one of the Lutyens-designed benches, Hugh says,

> It is essentially a rose garden, but we've tried to prolong the season by
> introducing flowering cherries and tulips – lily-flowered 'Triumphator'
> – among the lavender. It is a formal garden, and a degree of symmetry

*T*his closer view within the rose garden shows the all-important shape of the central feature, which is densely planted with lavender and surrounded by water to reflect the shapes. It also shows how the stone paving becomes a strong feature, with the pebbles set into cement, and a cool effect is given by the grass on each corner.

No Lutyens garden is complete without steps and seats. Architecturally designed steps on each corner lead gracefully to the slightly lower level, and you will find comfortable and well-designed seats to rest on. This picture clearly shows how the lines of the steps reflect those of the pool.

is essential. Here in the centre we have two different roses, pink 'Silver Jubilee' and scarlet-red 'Lilli Marlene', and round the outside are standard pink 'The Fairy', with 'Albéric Barbier' under it.

Other roses include 'Peace', 'Congratulations', 'Pink Perfection', the yellow 'Korresia' and the beautiful 'Camaïeux', whose white petals striped with pink are reminiscent of 'Rosa Mundi'. Gertrude Jekyll described 'The Fairy' in *Colour in the Flower Garden*:

> I have a little rose that I call the Fairy Rose. It came to me from a cottage garden, and I have never seen it elsewhere. It grows about a foot high and has blush-pink flowers with the colour deepening to the centre . . . It is an inch and a half across and of beautiful form, especially in the half-opened bud. Wishing to enjoy its beauty to the utmost, and to bring it comfortably within sight, I gave it a shelf in raised rock-work and brought near and under it a clear pale lilac Viola and a good drift of *Achillea umbellata*. It was worth doing.

You would think that this garden surrounded by yew hedges is well protected from the wind, but when it blows strongly it becomes a kind of hurricane – then the tops of the standard roses get bent and blown off.

KIFTSGATE COURT

*I*like to visit Kiftsgate as often in the year as possible, sure of discovering some special plant in flower at every season. In early July I know that the roses will be looking wonderful, the borders full and typically English.

On a summer visit you will be tempted to look at every plant in detail; do not be hurried – go either alone or with a like-minded friend, then you can make notes, take photographs and carry home ideas.

As you walk on to the terrace you will immediately be arrested by the sight of the huge *Magnolia delavayi* which covers a corner of the house wall. Heather Muir planted this fifty years ago and when you see its spread you will realize the number of summers it has given pleasure. Think of the future in your own garden, and plant likewise. This is a warm area, facing south and west, and I am always surprised how many shrubs survive here that would be too tender in our garden at Barnsley. There is a large *Ceanothus arborescens* 'Trewithen Blue', and *Lyonothamnus floribunda asplenifolius*, with beautiful evergreen leaves, deeply cut and fern-like; the creamy-white flowers open in clusters in early summer. *Rosa banksiae* 'Lutea' may have only a few remaining blooms, but *R. mutabilis* will be covered with flowers of varying colour and maturity.

Stone steps take you down to 'the four squares'. These are defined by paving and box and infilled with an inspired mixture of shrubs, roses and perennials. There is an unusual bush honeysuckle, which came from the late Countess Münster's garden at Bampton (you can buy it here). My special favourites are *Rodgersia pinnata* 'Superba', *Geranium* 'Buxton's Blue', *Aconitum napellus* 'Carnea' – a pinky-beige monkshood – spectacular *Heuchera cylindrica* 'Greenfinch', and *Cestrum parqui*. This cestrum is sometimes cut to the ground by frost but will always reappear. Look out for *Clematis* × *durandii*, *Pittosporum* 'Garnettii', and the Hybrid Tea rose 'Rita'. There are also lots of hebes, penstemons, erodiums, helianthemums, and many more roses. For accents of height Anne has groups of tall delphiniums and *Salvia candelabrum*. These plants and many others all work extremely well together: you will notice that the colours are kept to pinks, blues and purples, and reds on the blue side of the spectrum – in fact, there is no touch of yellow or orange.

Go down the steps on to the terrace overlooking the escarpment, where you can sit and take in the view. The two huge terracotta lemon pots – bought in Italy – are filled to overflowing with fuchsias, geraniums and *Melianthus major*. There is so much growing in them that they have to be fed regularly. On a hot summer's day it is good to walk on the grass path, softer than the paving for the feet, which takes you between the magnificent borders profusely planted with shrubs, roses and herbaceous things. There is plenty of height, provided by *Rosa highdownensis* and *R. rubrifolia* (*R. glauca*), *Photinia fraseri* 'Red Robin', potentillas, *Olearia nummularifolia* and a carpenteria. The shrubs form the shape and are backed up by asters,

*T*he white garden was originally designed by Mrs Muir fifty years ago, but other colours have slowly crept in. It is one of the most peaceful places to sit, using the wrought-iron seats – painted blue – to watch the water spraying from the central fountain. Diany found this well-head and had a replica made. The water sprays with the wind.

The planting is soft, using grasses, roses, deutzias, hoherias and hydrangeas. This garden covers all seasons of the year; enclosed by the house and yew hedges, it has a protected microclimate and the sun shines on it perpetually.

astrantia, crambe, lots of dianthus, penstemons and violas. Even though there is so much in these borders now, Anne assures me that there are also bulbs for spring, and fuchsias and later-flowering Michaelmas daisies to keep the colour interest through September and into October.

Before you reach the end of these borders turn right into the white sunken garden with its well-head and octagonal pool. The seats are painted a strong 'Trafalgar' blue, a daring colour to have chosen, but it certainly looks well. Sit quietly here and imagine how it could be a part of your own garden, and make notes of the planting. In summer the hostas provide enough foliage to offset the flowers of the campanulas, *Corydalis bulbosa*, the white dicentras, dictamnus and *Epilobium glabellum*. Make a note of the good combinations and more unusual edging plants – ophiopogon, *Phlox* 'Chattahoochee', different campanulas, sedums, and *Gentiana acaulis* and *G. asclepiades*.

Now is the time to see the famous Kiftsgate rose, bought by Heather Muir as *Rosa filipes*; when Graham S. Thomas saw it in 1951 he knew it was unique, and it was given its own name *R. filipes* 'Kiftsgate'. The other spectacle is the equally famous path edged with *Rosa gallica* 'Versicolor'. Some of these have sported back to the crimson parent, a touch of history. As you walk along the path you will find deutzias and astilbes. The focal point at the end, added by Diany Binney, is a seat made by Simon Verity

*T*his garden, initially designed by Mrs Muir, is elegantly simple – divided into four squares which give it its name, with a sundial as a central feature. The portico and the surrounding canopy of trees give height and shade, making this a pleasant place to walk in on hot summer days. It could be described as Mediterranean in feel, although the planting is of an English country garden at its most exuberant, with delphiniums, penstemons, many helianthemums, peonies, geraniums and daphnes. Terracotta pots filled with felicias and argyranthemums stand beside the blue-painted seat.

framed by an archway of *Sorbus aria* 'Lutescens'. Whichever way you look it has a quiet drama, with ferns, grasses, *Smilacina racemosa*, dwarf bamboos and hart's-tongue ferns. I find this view from the seat is a moment in time to catch and remember. You could copy it in your own garden.

The yellow border has a wonderful rhythm. There are three yellow acers, the 'Graham Thomas' roses, now 2 metres (7 ft) tall, the *Ligularia dentata* 'Desdemona' under the maples. I also noticed pale yellow hypericum with orange day lilies and yellow rock roses, *Ligularia przewalskii* under

*T*he famous Kiftsgate rose in flower as it starts its climb above the hedge of *Rosa gallica* 'Versicolor' and then reaches out into the pine trees. Anne Chambers assures me that they cannot get up to prune this rose so allow it a free range. It is usually in flower in early July and is indeed a spectacle of beauty.

On the right the Cotswold stone gable has a typical acute slant and an eighteenth-century drip-mould over the four-light window.

elaeagnus, and variegated-leaved astrantia. For more gold there is marjoram associated with *Euphorbia cyparissias*. Day lily 'Orange Chimes' and a bronze phormium – all spikes – contrast with the round heads of *Euphorbia characias*. Orange lilies have been dropped in between hypericums and round a *Euonymus japonicus*.

As I walk around the garden I list the plants which will self-seed – they are so useful, and will often put themselves into just the right place, or in crevices where it would be impossible to plant them. At Barnsley we have honesty, especially the white-flowered, variegated-leaved form, alliums of every species, canary creeper, and love-in-a-mist. In the vegetable garden we have some special hollyhocks and though we collect their seed we also scatter them, so that next year there will be a different picture. It is always exciting to allow seedlings to develop, you may have a different variety.

On a warm summer's day it is rewarding to walk down the steep bank to the lower garden. In a letter to me last year Anne wrote: 'Planting is a never ending occupation (as I'm sure you know). Johnny and I have concentrated on the lower garden over the past five years, and as it is so sheltered and we have had very mild winters we have managed to introduce lots of very tender plants, which so far have survived.' (This was written before the cold spells of early 1996.)

It is the most protected part of the garden, where even *Geranium palmatum* have become naturalized and abutilons have seeded themselves. Be sure to read Anne's booklet or you may miss some special buddleja, deutzia or roscoea not often grown but whose detail of colour is a living proof that nature can often do more for us than we can do for ourselves, if only, like Alice, we have time to listen.

*I*n the white sunk garden pairs of steps lead you gradually up and past borders filled with low-growing and scented plants – rock roses, campanulas, alliums, geraniums and lavender – towards the blue-painted door. Notice how the shape of the upright juniper echoes the curve of the door. The colours here are restful, but with accents of purple campanulas, turquoise hosta leaves and deep pink wild gladiolus so that the planting is never dull. ∾

*W*e all strive to have our containers filled with unusual plants, giving a bold effect. The secrets for success are to use plenty of plants so they will grow together, and then to feed them regularly. I recommend phostrogen.

Start with your central feature – here it is *Melianthus major* – then surround it with plants which will keep flowering throughout the summer and autumn: fuchsia, argyranthemums, helichrysums and parahebes. The colour scheme is bold and yet simple, red and green interspersed with grey. ∾

AUTUMN

I am thankful we have four distinct seasons, then we can appreciate the different moods of each. The choice of trees and shrubs for autumn colour will depend on the soil. If it is acid, fothergilla, enkianthus and most eucryphias flourish and colour well and trees like *Nyssa sylvatica*, *Stewartia serratta* and *S. sinensis* will turn brilliant colours.

In the lime (alkaline) soil at Barnsley we have planted several sorbus, mountain ash, and these make beautiful displays with their berries and autumn colour. Sorbus have white, pink, yellow and red berries and in autumn you will discover which berries are first to ripen, for the birds will naturally go to these. With us the white and pink-tinged berries of *Sorbus hupehensis* stay on well after the leaves have fallen and so do the fruits on the crabs *Malus toringoides* and *M. transitoria*.

We have been working hard on planting herbaceous flowers which will keep blooming well into October. These are the Compositae heleniums, helianthus and heliopsis as well as the annual sunflowers. Many of the salvias do not come into flower until autumn and the varied lobelias are the same. Sometimes I wish that autumn would last longer.

*T*here are moments in the exotic garden at Great Dixter when the colour scheme is more traditional. *Verbena bonariensis* appears everywhere, and the drooping flowers of white *Nicotiana sylvestris* echo the leaves of the tall grass, *Arundo donax*.

Cannas and phormium leaves spire towards the chimneys of the house. This new garden, enclosed by the old yew hedges planted by Nathaniel Lloyd, was originally known as the tropical garden, but so much is actually hardy that Christopher Lloyd has decided to call it the exotic garden. Walking around it with Christo is an enlivening experience.

GREAT DIXTER

*E*very year autumn is different. Sometimes it comes on us in a tremendous rush, and an early frost catches us unawares before all our tender plants have been given their winter protection. One day I may walk round my garden at Barnsley thinking how perfect the lobelias, salvias and dahlias all look, then overnight the scene changes dramatically: a hard frost has blackened the dahlias, and the lobelias and salvias have lost their pristine charm.

Fortunately, frost does not often occur in the Cotswolds as early as September, so our borders go on looking well structured and colourful for several more weeks. One year we had a frost on 28 September, but it did not hit us again until 9 and 10 November. According to my garden diary, the first hard frost came on 17 November another year; in 1992 the first ground frost was on 15 October, and in 1995 our first, very mild, frost was on 28 October. So, you see, you cannot rely on the diary for frost dates – you must study the sky, the clouds and the feel of the temperature, as well as the moon, and become your own weatherman. It is often the clouds which give the weather prophet the most useful clues.

In September and October, as through the rest of the year, every detail must be cared for. Dying flowers, if allowed to remain on the plant, will produce seeds to provide a feast for garden birds and migrants, or to be collected and sown for a future display – or maybe they will self-sow. My loyalties are divided. Nature is very generous with her gifts and we must reciprocate.

Hopefully by September the watering cans and hosepipes will be less in demand as the need for watering tubs and pots reduces, but another daily routine will soon be on us: leaf-fall starts gently in September, rising to a crescendo in October and November; by December all our deciduous trees should be bare, allowing the evergreens to come into their own and give the winter garden its own structure.

*A*utumn in the peacock garden. The wide edgings of *Aster lateriflorus* 'Horizontalis' link the topiary peacocks each side of the stone path. This aster is covered with small flowers with a purple boss and whitish rays.

The firm structure of yews in this garden is dramatic, and seen from this position they echo the shape of the oast-house roofs in the distance. Nathaniel Lloyd loved the art of topiary, and he had the idea of this bird topiary, each one poised on top of a pyramidal yew plinth. Christo's mother called them a 'Parliament of birds'.

Last September I thought our borders at Barnsley were doing well in spite of the drought and the fawn lawns. We had penstemons, monardas, lobelias, phlox, lots of violas and everlasting sweet peas, sunflowers and rudbeckias, among others. Then, early in the month, I went to Christopher Lloyd's garden at Great Dixter. As I walked round his borders with him, my pride-bubble burst. I like to think our borders are planted in layers so there is a succession of plants in bloom through most of the year: the Dixter borders looked much like ours, but were definitely more interesting, and Christo had the edge on us with his clever use of unusual annuals and biennials. These, if dead-headed, give a longer display than most perennials, but they take more time, thought and work. Christo had generous clumps of *Tithonia rotundifolia* 'Torch', *Ageratum* 'Blue Horizon', *Zinnia linarifolia* 'Orange Star' and white cosmos, which he had grown specially to follow on after the lupins.

Christo says 'Spring happens', but we must plan and work for a good display in summer and through autumn. For example the lupins (treated as biennials), which flowered with such effect in early summer are dug up and

*I*n autumn the evening sun on the peacock garden highlights the flowering sprays of *Miscanthus sinensis* 'Silver Feather'. Through and behind them bright orange *Canna* 'Wyoming' make a picture with the yellow *Helianthus salicifolius*, pink *Aster lateriflorus* 'Horizontalis' and cream pampas grass, *Cortaderia selloana* 'Pumila'.

replaced with penstemons, verbenas, or with his summer-flowering annuals. All this is very labour-intensive, especially when there is a ready back-up supply of plants lined up waiting to fill the spaces and revitalize the borders. Christo advises that before you move any plants you give them a good soaking, replant them and then re-soak them in their new home.

That was the first lesson I learnt on my September day at Dixter: Nick Burton, my new head gardener, must study the seed catalogues to increase our repertoire of annuals. It is simple to sow pans of seeds early in the year, but time-consuming to prick them out and pot them on. Remember there is no need to prick out more seedlings than you will need in your own garden – you can always give the remaining young seedlings in their pan to a gardening friend.

A cheering thought for keen gardeners is that Christo uses cold frames (no artificial heat) to bring on these plants.

This master gardener always has an ace up his sleeve, and his new planting in the old rose garden will I'm sure influence many English country gardeners (the trend of the late 1990s?): now in its third season, it has been transformed into a tropical delight. Christo and Fergus have created this startling paradise in a space enclosed by old yew hedges on three sides, and by a red-roofed barn on the other side. In winter the beds are flat, almost empty, then by the end of May planting begins afresh.

The structure of paths and hedges designed by Sir Edwin Lutyens remains from the rose garden era, but the 'new' concept of planting harks back to the nineteenth century, to William Robinson and Shirley Hibberd. This reinforces my belief that there is little new in the tradition of our English country gardens. We have used the same recurring themes for centuries, but now a much wider variety of plants – some imported, some 'improved' – is available to us.

To quote from Shirley Hibberd's *Rustic Adornments for Homes of Taste,* published in 1872:

> A great number of plants of most noble proportions, many of them gaily coloured, and when lacking colour making ample amends by the splendour of their leafage, may be made perfectly at home in our gardens during the summer . . . Perhaps the first place in this glorious company should be assigned to the Cannas . . . These are just as easy to grow as dahlias . . . The Yuccas, Agave, Bamboos, the *Papyrus antiquorum*, afford fine masses for suitable positions.

We probably associate William Robinson with his strong influence, at the end of the nineteenth century, on the change from the bedding-out of high Victorian times to more natural gardens, herbaceous borders, wild-flower meadows and woodland planting. We overlook the fact that as a young gardener in the 1860s he spent time in Paris as correspondent of *The Times*; in his exhilarating book *The Parks, Promenades and Gardens of Paris* he

*F*rom roses to exotics is a dramatic change. When Fergus arrived as head gardener, Christo took out his rose garden and has allowed his imagination a full range to make an unusual garden with tropical, half-hardy plants and others with bold leaves.

In this picture the red *Dahlia* 'Wittemans Superb' and the variegated leaves of *Canna malawiensis* 'Variegata' are a good contrast. Elsewhere the bold foliage of banana plants, castor oils, cannas, Egyptian papyrus and the *Paulownia tomentosa* stooled back by Christo, give the garden a very exotic feel. To the left, the late-flowering *Escallonia bifida* attracts every butterfly in the neighbourhood.

devotes a long chapter to 'Subtropical Plants for the Flower Garden'. His explanation of 'subtropical' is

> the introduction of a rich and varied vegetation, chiefly distinguished by beauty of form . . . The system had its origin in Paris, (then) Mr Gibson, the able and energetic superintendent of Battersea Park . . . boldly tried the system, and with what a result all know who have seen his charming 'subtropical garden' in Battersea Park.

William Robinson goes on to recommend agaves, aralias, ferns, cannas, echeveria, nicotiana, solanums. A study of this chapter is well worth while.

I do not know if Christo has been influenced by these two writers, but it illustrates the natural recurrence of fashion – an interesting thought, and also applicable to clothes, architecture and interior design. Recently I have been reading Vivian Russell's book about Monet's colour thoughts and his garden at Giverny. We could all follow his example, using some of his ideas to enliven our gardens through the whole year.

To return to Great Dixter, where exciting exotics pervade: cannas, some with especially handsome and well-veined leaves, are treated in groups, not as the 'dot plants' of urban park beds. Castor-oil plants have grown 1.8 metres (6 ft) tall from seed in a season. There are carefully chosen dahlias – the most elegant-flowered varieties combined with good foliage. Kniphofias sparkle between the banana plants, Japanese musa, and the huge leaves of *Paulownia tomentosa*, and the tree of heaven, *Ailanthus altissima*, both of which are stooled back every spring to create this surprising leaf effect. I was excited by the *Nicotiana glauca* – a wonderful grey foliage with a not-so-significant yellow flower.

It was the early autumn light showing up this eclectic collection of plants which gripped my attention – in autumn, as in spring, all leaves have such a diversity of veining. I was spellbound, and so were the bees, butterflies and hover flies homing in on the verbenas, especially *V. bonariensis*, the 'see-through' plant. I felt that I was in an unfamiliar forest – the top storey of paulownia and ailanthus, the understorey of bananas and cannas, the ground cover of kniphofia and cosmos. This was an experience not to be missed, especially walking through with its creator, who murmured, 'I feel there may be tigers and parrots round the next corner – I hope they're more friendly than the roses were.'

Christo experienced roses as tyrants, dictators – demanding attention, only sticks in winter – so decided to uproot them. His new garden reaches a crescendo of exuberance, of flowers as well as foliage, all through the late summer months. When nature is kind, this display carries on into October, and sometimes into November. We must always make the most of late summer and autumn days. Christo does so, and his garden is still full of colour – backed up by many different greens.

Just because the 'old rose garden' with its new 'exotics' was so exciting

The eye-catching orange-red kniphofia is the centre of attraction in this view of the long border in very early autumn. It contrasts with the column of purple *Clematis* 'Jackmanii Superba' and blends with the spikes of the yellow mulleins. Nearby, but not in this picture, is the orange-flowered annual *Tithonia* 'Torch'. For height, the cardoons tower above the pink tamarisk on one side, and on the other Christo has *Gleditsia triacanthos* 'Elegantissima' with its delicate leaves to create a division. The pink of the tamarisk is repeated near the front, using *Rosa* 'The Fairy' and border phloxes.

I must not neglect to browse along Christo's famous long border. This is a perfect example, one where you must always spend time walking both ways. You will then see plants at a different angle and in different associations of colour, texture and shape.

At the back of the long border, which is brilliant for at least eight months of the year, the taller plants – 'Golden King' holly, gleditsia, tamarisk and cardoons – provide a solid, effective backdrop. As well as the annuals I've mentioned earlier, there are pools of colour, with red *Salvia microphylla* var. *neurepia* – cuttings must be taken of this as it is not reliably hardy. *Lavatera olbia*, flowering continuously since July, echoes the pink of autumn colchicums, and the white variety, *Colchicum speciosum* 'Album', grow through *Helichrysum petiolare* 'Variegatum'. The late-blooming *Kniphofia* 'Torchbearer' are outstanding with the afternoon sun shining through them.

At the border's edge are the South African bulbs, *Zephyranthes candida*, white flowers emerging through dark green, rush-like leaves. Another from South Africa is the rich red *Schizostylis coccinea* 'Major'; *S. c.* 'Viscountess Byng' flowers later. I have always resisted buying these bulbs, wondering if they would perform for me in my alkaline soil. Christo is most positive about them and recommends the pale pink 'Pallida', salmon-pink 'Sunset', and also 'Alba', so I will be planting all of these to give life to my September borders.

Closer to the house was a wonderful *Hebe* 'Jewel', and teasels had been allowed to self-sow as volunteers among the lace-cap hydrangeas, the asters and the vibrant *Geranium* 'Ann Folkard' and the hardy fuchsias which Christo has nurtured to make a surprising autumn showing.

Each season must have its crescendo, and it is we who can orchestrate this in our gardens.

In a south-west corner near the house, several hydrangeas flourish, some lace-cap and others mopheads. They all like a well-manured soil with a moist root-run. The white is *H. paniculata* 'Tardiva', the pink, *H. macrophylla* 'Nigra' and the purple, *H. m.* 'Blue Wave'. They are backed up in front with dahlia seedlings which are never lifted, and the 'see-through' *Verbena bonariensis*. The giant reed grass, *Arundo donax*, gives a good background, and nearby Christo has hardy fuchsias for his autumn display.

HOLKER HALL

The woodland at Holker is exciting in every month of the year. The monkey puzzle, *Araucaria araucana*, is now 151 years old, its long spidery branches spoked out above its distinctive trunk. Seed was brought back to Holker from Chile, and when it was forty years old the tree was blown down in a gale. It took seven shire horses to re-erect it (and how many men?) There are seven of its 'seedling' trees in the upper woodland garden.

At the same time, Lord Burlington was enlarging the garden and making the fountain; then, and through to the present day, estate labour has always been used for every possible project. The surround of the fountain is cobblestones, incorporating a snake and porcupine, designed by Grania and both made using 'off-cuts' of waste from the industry developed from the slate quarries on the estate. The family crest includes a snake in the figure of eight, but why the porcupine? – maybe a Sienese *contrados* (the Cavendishes often visit Tuscany). Nearby is the largest cut-leaf beech I have ever seen. Its trunk, like the prow of a ship, is dramatic – but difficult to photograph.

The statue of Inigo Jones standing on a plinth of Burlington slate is made of lead, after a stone original by Rysbrack, and came from Chiswick House in London. Turn right here under a stone archway for a longer walk, or left for a shorter meander. We will take the long way, to look at many of the shrubs planted by Hugh's grandmother. You must take your copy of Hugh's 'Woodland Gardens Guide' with you, as he has wisely numbered his trees and shrubs rather than name them, so that visitors will not be tempted to remove labels. Be sure to take a notebook too.

The understorey planting is interesting, with *Garrya elliptica* from California and pittosporums from New Zealand and Australia. The

In the woodland garden, when you reach the statue of Inigo Jones, you can make the decision to go by the Cavendish Walk, taking a leisurely hour and a half, or to take a shorter one-hour route – the Burlington Walk.

Inigo Jones stands on his plinth of local slate, shaded by the tulip tree, *Liriodendron tulipifera*. It flowers in June and July and has a distinctive leaf that is turning a strong buttercup yellow this autumn. The statue is lead, after a stone original by Rysbrack, which the 7th Duke of Devonshire brought from his London home at Chiswick House.

Turn right past an archway in a drystone wall for the longer walk, and left for a shorter meander that is more suitable for wheelchairs.

snowdrop tree, *Halesia carolina*, has white hanging bell-shaped flowers in May, winged fruits in winter. On the cornus bank there is a collection of dogwoods, mostly planted by Hugh since 1986. It is a good example of the continuity in planting here: each generation of the family has maintained the flow of young trees and shrubs, adding where there is space, and clearing away and carefully pruning when necessary.

The planting mostly 'lines' the pathways, but sometimes you must make your way 'in the bushes'. Planted in one off-shoot of the main paths are robinias, gleditsias and caragana, all members of the same pea family, and

*S*pring, when the leaf buds are opening, and autumn, as the leaves turn to golds and crimson, are dramatic times in the woodland. The mature trees were planted in the nineteenth century by Cavendish ancestors including the 7th Duke of Devonshire, later by Lady Moyra Cavendish and now, more recently, by Hugh Cavendish. I was impressed by the layout, as shrubs and trees have not been crowded

all imported from the United States of America since the seventeenth century. Growing with these is an unusual whitebeam; the *Sorbus aria* are English natives, but this specimen has especially large leaves. In spring their undersides are strikingly silvery-grey, and before they open fully the leaves could be mistaken for magnolia flowers.

The path takes you along the boundary wall, and Hugh and his predecessors have made the most of this sheltered place. The New Zealand kowhai, *Sophora tetraptera*, and the Japanese bitter orange, *Poncirus trifoliata*, thrive here – beware of the fierce thorns on the poncirus, whence its other common name, crown of thorns.

Two other shrubs with interesting features are the *Staphylea holocarpa* 'Rosea', with fruits contained in inflated parchment-coloured bladders, earning it the name bladder-nut; and *Decaisnea fargesii* from west China has large pinnate leaves, sometimes 1 metre (3 ft) long, with yellow flowers in 50 cm (20 in) racemes; these produce metallic blue pods which hang on the branches like beans through autumn and well into winter.

By this time you may be wanting a rest – especially if it is the end of the day. Most thoughtfully, a seat awaits you, made of slate 'clog'; clog is the term used by local quarrymen to describe the blocks of slate in the form they are 'won' from the hillside. Continuity again, for the Cavendish family has been working slate quarries around here for more than two hundred years.

You will see on your left, as you pause a while on the seat, the seven 'children' of the large monkey puzzle. Interestingly, each has its own individual characteristics, a slight variation in bark and overall shape. Either side of the monkey puzzle grove are two magnolias, *M. × loebneri* 'Merrill' and *M. × l.* 'Leonard Messel', both derived from the same parentage, a cross between *M. kobus* and *M. stellata* which originated at Nymans in Sussex, an important garden made by the late Colonel Lionel Messel.

A vast oak held my attention – it is the Hungarian oak, *Quercus frainetto*, with a very fissured bark; the leaves are deeply lobed. At this moment I thought what a lot horticultural students could learn from walking with Hugh through his woodland at every season, tracing the history of the introduction from all over the world of rhododendrons, azaleas, magnolias, viburnums and others; they would also come to appreciate how long it takes for trees to reach maturity and flowering age, and the importance of grouping some genera while allowing others to stand as isolated trees in order to reveal their full beauty.

There are moments in my mind which will never fade. Here at Holker it will be the sight of the monkey puzzle, the hanging catkins on the *Pterocarya fraxinifolia*, the wing-nut tree, the trunk of the cut-leaf beech, the davidia's large white bracts, and *Rosa omeiensis pteracantha* (*R. sericea* var. *pteracantha*) with the setting sun, low in the evening sky, glowing through its red thorns.

together – they are spaced to give each specimen a full spread, allowing for underplanting in the shade of the trees.

In the foreground of this picture a well-branched acer will soon lose its leaves, and behind, an evergreen provides winter texture and an architectural statement. ❧

CHILCOMBE HOUSE

The twin mixed borders either side of the main axis in the walled garden at Chilcombe still look full in September in spite of having given of their best earlier in the year (it is easy for borders to be blowsy by then). John successfully drops grasses in pots into the gaps, and acanthus complements groups of salvias – *S. spathacea*, the pitcher sage, the blue *S. syphilitica*, and a favourite of mine, *S. uliginosa*.

The advice John gives freely to aspiring gardeners who want the maximum effect from spring to autumn is to plant closely and then, to prevent plants flopping over, stake them with hazel sticks early enough – the growing perennials will soon merge into them. Connect small areas with arches, vistas, a rhythm of plants and a continuity of path pattern. A garden should be relaxed so that it does not overwhelm you, a place where you can overhear visitors saying, 'We could do this at home.'

Chilcombe rarely has frost, so tender plants keep flowering on into October; by then it is the shorter days with fewer hours of light which influence their behaviour. The climbing roses and honeysuckles will no longer distract our attention with their luxuriance; we can see more clearly through the arches into the next compartment, and appreciate how John always has in mind a tapestry of muted tones – pink and grey – and colours which are complementary, such as blue and yellow, deep purple, rich blues and orange.

He admits, 'I love municipal parks with their bedding-out but this is not what we are trying to do, because this garden is basically cottagey'.

When the Hubbards explained to their first gardener where they planned to have the sundial and herb garden, his immediate reaction was, 'Oh dear! it's the best place for carrots.' They still have carrots, now growing in Caryl's vegetable garden at the lower end of the slope and the erstwhile 'best place for carrots' is a successful formal sundial garden at the top end. This is surrounded by sage, followed by a lawn, and then borders – it reminds me of John's pictures. The central path is edged with 'Hidcote' lavender.

From here a narrow – dare I say precipitous? – path takes you past one end of the holly and beech alley and then beside a red, black and white currant hedge. Nearby is a rather daring patch of late-flowering salvias, *S. involucrata* 'Bethellii', pale fuchsia and *S. madrensis* with yellow flowers and large leaves. *Rehmannia elata* is doing well in nearby borders. In Gloucestershire I keep this indoors, but as it increases by adventitious roots it prefers an unrestricted space to a 25 cm (10 in) pot. John says he wants to introduce more good evergreen shrubs – so in winter he and Caryl will see them from their windows.

John and I both like the combination of blue and yellow, expanded to mauve and orange. At Barnsley we have this in spring with forget-me-nots and yellow tulips, while John has it in September with blue felicia and

The garden on the north side of the house is different in character from the rest of the garden. It is bounded on one side by a wooded bank and the old ice house, and enclosed on the other by the farmhouse. The wild flower garden is nearby, reached through a stone archway.

You can sit here peacefully to enjoy the Dorset countryside and then browse around to discover the wide selection of ferns – those native to the Hubbards' own woodland, and others John has brought in. They all thrive on this soil, shaded from the midday sun.

Every garden should have a surprise, and this is Chilcombe's.

golden bidens, and the very special annual *Lobelia* 'Victoria', with purple stems matching its purple flowers.

John expressed to me how he often uses a 'ground' colour when planting – just like the preliminary wash or the ground in a picture, or the continuo in music. For example, he scatters double violet *Geranium pratense* throughout his double border so that everything else emerges from it. 'When you look at the work of a master colourist such as Manet, you find on closer inspection that the actual colours used are few and usually very subtle. They function by association rather than brute force.' I so agree, and would add green, which many people forget is itself an important, and highly varied, colour.

John, an American by birth, was also influenced by the garden he had as a child. 'My parents sent me out with packets of seed. A garden is a place where one is happy, and gardening is fun, not work. Because I am a painter, where concentration is important, gardening is an after-hours pleasure.' I was impressed by my new gardening friend's artist's eye, and the way he has naturally transposed his imagination from canvas to garden.

HELMINGHAM HALL

It is often colder in autumn in Suffolk than in the West Country, but in kind years the penstemons will still be flowering in the Helmingham borders, and so will the diascias, the osteospermums, *Salvia uliginosa* and several abutilons; until the dahlias – Xa's favourite is 'Arabian Nights' – are hit by frost it seems that autumn may at last join hands with spring.

The knots look beautiful in every season, especially in winter when frost or snow lights up the pattern of the threads; and in spring when many of the early bulbs are pushing through. In summer and autumn, your gaze will be towards the roses.

The Hybrid Musk roses are flowering for a second time. There are autumn crocus, and a line of *Nerine bowdenii* stretching along half the south-facing wall of the potager, wonderful for cutting for the house. From the potager cauliflowers, spinach, beetroot, and carrots come in daily, and the delicious Conference pears as they ripen. In the main herbaceous borders there is a wealth of flowers and colour; many plants, such as penstemons, cosmos and dahlias, will recover from a dry summer to produce a second offering of flower, while *Aster* × *frikartii* 'Mönch', sedums and *Anemone japonica* are giving their usual autumn display, as are the crinum lilies. I only wish that the late-flowering salvias, *S. greggii* and *S.* var. *neurepia*, would do as well every year as they did after the hot summer of 1995.

It is always important to make notes of our failures – how else can we improve? Last year our gourds at Barnsley, like those at Helmingham, were weaker, not so vigorous and spectacular. Perhaps they did not get their roots deep down before the hot weather set in, or did we fail them with not enough manure?

The herbaceous borders each side of the central grass path are still full of colour. There are annuals – *Scabiosa* 'Black Ball', godetia, clarkia and tall *Nicotiana sylvestris*. *Choisya ternata* is in full bloom, its orange-blossom scent vying with the sweet fragrance of *Viburnum* × *bodnantense*.

A dramatic, unforgettable scene in the walled vegetable garden – a tunnel of gourds. The narrowness of the path and the size of the bench at the end make you wonder if you have stepped with Alice into the White Rabbit's tunnel. I must congratulate the grower on the diversity of shapes, sizes and colours, and ask him the secret of his success. If you have no tunnel, try growing them on a trellis or up a pyramid of bamboo.

Nature's game of bowls – by autumn the pears will be falling and must be picked up before the mowing can be done. The pears are delicious when cooked but are not good eaters.

In the picture on the left petunias and white nicotiana give colour to the parterre beds as the Hybrid Musk roses finish flowering. The parterres are now planted with santolina, but the white nicotiana has been retained. The mellow brick walls give a feeling of privacy, and the simple seats are far enough apart from each other for you to feel alone when sitting on them.

The picture below is a reminder to all gardeners not to neglect the autumn bulbs. These colchicums come as a special surprise when the flowers push through without their leaves. What, I wonder, should we plant them with? I think they would be dramatic between hostas or *Sedum spectabile*. Here they are planted under the old pear tree and have probably been growing and multiplying for years.

One of the joys of an exceptional autumn, as Xa remarks, is to be able to arrange roses, dahlias, even delphiniums and penstemons, for the dining-room table – an August arrangement in October. Last autumn *Clematis* 'Comtesse de Bouchard' was making a late display on the wall, and *C. cirrhosa* 'Freckles', usually blooming in December and January, was already in full flower. Each year is different, the seasons so variable that plants sometimes mistake one for another.

There are vegetables as well as flowers to bring in for the table – spinach, cauliflowers, beetroot and Brussels sprouts – and a bounty of fruit – pears, especially Conference, plums and apples. Figs are more temperamental: the trees on the east-facing wall did well in the heat of 1995, but those facing south found that exceptional summer *too* hot. 'Hooray, hooray,' Xa wrote to me last October, 'it has rained and the park is green again.' The autumn colour was late last year, but soon the sorbus and liquidambar, *Prunus serrulata* and amelanchier were aflame, and the crab apples, *Malus* 'Golden Hornet', were so laden with fruit that the branches were pendulous.

WINFIELD HOUSE

Many of our familiar evergreen trees in Britain have reached us from the Pacific North-West – the western red cedar, the Wellingtonia, the Douglas fir, and many of the pines; in fact, 60 per cent of the conifers listed in that useful reference book *The Plant Finder* come from the United States, and there are almost as many deciduous trees. The robinia, or false acacia, is native to middle and eastern America, and there are many dogwoods (cornus), several magnolias and the tulip tree (liriodendron). Then there are the annuals and perennials without which our borders would be dull, especially in summer and autumn. Many have been planted at Winfield House, and can also be seen in most English country gardens.

The summer impression of overall green-ness surrounding the house has changed by October and early November. The lawn is still immaculate and verdant but, as the head gardener Stephen Crisp says, 'The garden is really given a boost by the North American species that we have planted, particularly since 1983.' It is so important to have spectacular distant views from the windows of this house, and from the terrace on the south front. As you walk through the woodland garden you can see the detail of these trees and shrubs with their underplanting.

Ambassador and Mrs Price from Kansas City, in residence from 1983 to 1989, planted the American sweet gum, *Liquidambar styraciflua*, an imposing tree with leaves resembling a maple's and colouring in autumn to a strong crimson. The liquidambars thrive best on an acid soil, so do not do well in my Cotswold garden or in chalk gardens, but at Winfield House they are spectacular by November.

President Bush's visit in 1989 is commemorated by an oak, the pin oak, *Quercus palustris*, a fast-growing deciduous tree from the east coast, first introduced to England *circa* 1800. It is elegant, the leaves often turning a rich crimson in autumn. Another visitor, Vice-President Al Gore, presented and planted a red oak, *Quercus rubra*, a fast-growing tree which again is tolerant of a town atmosphere. The contribution of Ambassador Henry Catto (1989–1991) is a Shumard oak, a deciduous tree with a rather smooth bark, less deeply furrowed than our English oak. More recently Ambassador and Mrs Seitz planted an *Amelanchier canadensis*, with white spring blossom and vivid but brief autumn colour, while President Clinton marked his visit on 29 November 1995 by planting the Arkansas water oak.

Another outstanding tree making a wonderful bronze-yellow autumn contribution is the deciduous swamp cypress, *Taxodium distichum*. This has reddish-brown bark and a buttressed trunk. Although traditionally grown in damp, swampy ground and a dominant tree in the Everglades region of Florida, it is suited to our English climate and has become a familiar tree growing by park lakes and even town ponds. The specimens at Winfield House are tall and imposing.

$\mathcal{M}$ature trees give Winfield a park-like grandeur. Some date from the nineteenth century, but many have been planted since the house became the residence of the American Ambassadors to the Court of St James's. Here, *Taxodium distichum* was planted in the 1970s – the evening sun highlights individual branches and throws strong shadows on the lawn. Young trees also play an important role. Those on the hill on the left were planted by Stephen Crisp in 1988 and include chestnuts and European beech.

A tall North American tulip tree, *Liriodendron tulipifera*, is doing well, the flowers opening in June and the unusually shaped leaves becoming butter-yellow in autumn. Nearby, the Indian Bean tree, *Catalpa bignonioides*, has foxglove-like flowers in July; with its huge leaves it is best in a place out of the wind. A star turn in October and November is the stag's-horn sumach, *Rhus typhina*, with leaves changing to vivid red, crimson and yellow.

All these American species help to enliven the 'fall' colour. But we must never forget the berries, and here at Winfield are many species of

*T*hroughout summer the roses scent the air in the second, more informal, rose garden designed by Sir Peter Shepherd with roses chosen by Nancy-Mary Goodall. The central feature is a rounded archway covered with *R. banksiae* 'Lutea' and *R.* 'The Garland' and underplanted with *R.* 'The Fairy'. Herbaceous perennials spill over the path, and in winter *Nepeta mussinii* and bergenia disguise the bare stems of the roses. Looking out of the rose garden, the focal point framed by the leaning sides of the clipped yew hedge is the pin oak, *Quercus palustris*, officially planted by President George Bush in June 1989.

pyracantha – the suitably named firethorn – with a choice of berries from rich yellow through orange-yellow and orange-red to the scarlet fruits of *P. atalantioides*. Crataegus, our own native hawthorn, provide that English look, while *C. crus-gallii*, the cockspur thorn from east and central America, planted in an avenue alongside the drive five years ago, gives a wonderful display of white blossom, autumn colour and long-lasting berries. One of Stephen Crisp's favourite small trees is *C. prunifolia*, planted near his own house in the grounds. This hawthorn is broad-headed, with very showy red fruits which last well into winter, hanging on long after the richly coloured autumn leaves have fallen.

Many hollies were planted in the late 1930s, at the time when the American heiress Barbara Hutton built the house. These hollies, now mature, contribute handsome berries – so useful for winter decorations in the house, culminating in the Christmas festivities.

Charles Sprague Sargent, director of the Arnold Arboretum in Boston for many years from 1872, is commemorated at Winfield House by two ornamental trees. *Prunus sargentii* is one of the loveliest of cherries, with single pink flowers in late March; the leaves start bronze-red in spring, become green, then finally in autumn turn a vibrant orange and crimson. This cherry was brought back from China by Ernest Henry Wilson, who was sent there, first by the English firm of Veitch and Son then, in 1907–8, sponsored by the Arnold Arboretum. He worked with Charles Sprague Sargent for many years, producing an account of the plants he had collected, among them this prunus.

Sorbus sargentiana is one of the most beautiful of the mountain ash tribe, again introduced by E. H. Wilson (in 1908) and named for his sponsor, C. S. Sargent. The winter buds are crimson and sticky, the leaves large with several slender, pointed leaflets, but it is the great clusters of red fruits in October and November which are outstanding.

In this 'country garden in London' you will sometimes find plenty of flowers still in bloom in November, due to the microclimate. The late-flowering roses are especially welcome – 'Margaret Merril', 'Iceberg' and 'Jacqueline du Pré'.

High summer cares for itself – it is the thoughtful gardener who carries on the interest later into the year. Iona loves visiting other gardens, and I was impressed by her selective choice of plants for autumn. As well as roses, she has penstemons, lobelias, hydrangeas, tall grasses, a selection of asters and drifts of cyclamen.

The trees are changing colour as I walk into Peter's sculpture garden. Shrubs, even evergreens, change through the seasons, but sculptures are static. I believe this garden's theme may have started as a whim – Peter may not agree. It happened like this, four years ago. The Carringtons got rid of the house cows, so the paddock where these once grazed needed a new purpose. A bulldozer came in for two days, accentuating the bumps to produce a piece of undulating ground. Robert Adams made a plan for a sort of lake, but that was no good – why have a lake on high ground. 'The people in the village thought we were building a golf course.'

At this point Iona, who did not like the idea of a new garden – it would be too much work – confronted Peter, who said, literally off the top of his head, 'It's going to be a sculpture garden.' Iona retorted rather acidly, 'Well, you haven't got any sculptures.' 'So we had to set about getting some.'

Around the existing trees Iona and Robert Adams designed and planted up island beds with shrubs, many of them evergreen. The shrubs have now grown up – and the sculptures have arrived. Peter asked the Professor of Sculpture at the Royal College of Art to bring some students down, and the result was two sculptures – a marble lady lying on her stomach, by Paul Vanstone, and an intriguing slate paving by Alistair Lambert. But my eye was immediately caught by a gorilla: the work of Michael Cooper, he is a great presence, and a friendly guardian.

Most of the sculptures chosen by Peter are representational – the marble lady lying on her stomach, the tumblers and the three fruits. Here is my favourite piece, an abstract bronze interpretation of Immortality made by the Australian sculptor John Robinson. It is a continuous ribbon with the light playing on the flowing surfaces, viewed from every angle and rotating on its pedestal. It is at the top of the garden so needs to be searched for – greatly satisfying when you come upon it. I hope one day that Peter will find a more deserving pedestal than the present brick pier. The borders around are massed with shrubs chosen for their flowers and autumn colour. ✂

Peter's most recent venture, started in 1992, is the sculpture garden, on undulating ground and with shrub borders planted by Iona to provide year-long interest.

Your attention immediately focuses on this reclining gorilla carved by Michael Cooper. He has a friendly presence and gives the feeling that he is guarding the place. His tiny ear and human-sized eyes might make it hard for him to detect an intruder, but his strong arms, hands and jaw are poised for action. He is resting on square stones, set on, and surrounded by, moss-covered bricks – a good place to sit, look around and touch his tactile torso. ✂

Then you find the two tumblers. Patrick Barker told Peter that he had been longing for some time to carve figures somersaulting down a bank, and here is the ideal place – the contour of the ground is like a shallow bowl, with shrubs on three sides, ideal for these arresting stone tumblers, not quite lifelike but with a strength and human meaning. One of them is landing, and his feet and a big toe stick up; you feel you must quickly touch the tumblers, before they somersault completely. Will they roll further down the slope when you turn your back? – who knows?

Move on and you will find three fruits, by Peter Randall-Page – a pomegranate, a pumpkin and a gourd, just the right size for children to sit on under the beech tree. My favourite piece in this garden, however – immensely satisfying aesthetically – is not representational. By the Australian sculptor John Robinson, 'Immortality' is made of a continuous ribbon of bronze which you can rotate on its pedestal.

BARNSLEY HOUSE

I love these months – as late summer finally settles to melt into autumn, the dew on the grass demands gumboots, and the intricate tracery of the hundreds of spiders' webs on the evergreens demands attention. Theirs is a transient beauty, easy to miss unless you are up betimes – they disappear from sight as the dewdrops dry.

The best light in the garden is in autumn and spring, when the sun is low in the sky. Long shadows on the lawn give a different dimension from their shorter midsummer shapes. On clear autumn mornings the sky will often be intensely blue, and the slowly moving white clouds create a feeling of calm – not the feeling of urgency that I have in March when the wind is blowing and the emerging leaves are competing for attention.

Before winter finally sets in, we will have magic moments of autumn colour. We work hard to give our gardens good spring blossom and plenty of summer flowers, but autumn colour is a bonus we may not always have planned for, and it varies in intensity each year. In the mixed borders, if there have been no hard frosts, the late flowerers carry on for extra, stolen days, golden helianthus and richly coloured asters holding up their heads among the hosta leaves as these turn buttercup-yellow. (The stems and foliage of *Euphorbia griffithii* 'Dixter' daily become more intensely red and delight me as they bend over the exotic late-flowering trycertis.)

I was amazed by my long list of flowers still in bloom on 25 October last year, 1995. The star turn was *Lobelia syphilitica*, a pale but strong blue, 80 cm (2½ feet) tall, with good foliage. The other lobelias, *L. cardinalis* and *L.* 'Flamingo', were over. There were salvias, the herbaceous yellow *Salvia glutinosa* and the pale blue *S. uliginosa*, and the pale *S.* 'Cambridge Blue' challenging the dark Oxford blue *S. patens*. Astrantias, diascias and nicotianas were still looking fresh, having carried on throughout the summer, especially *N. langsdorffii* and *N. sylvestris*.

We expect the asters to dominate in the September/October borders, but when *Geranium* 'Ann Folkard' has *Viola* 'Belmont Blue' climbing through it, near *Physostegia virginiana* 'Vivid', this border seems to belong more to July than to October. On the corners of the other beds are erodiums, lamium and *Nemesia umbonata* (now called *N. fruticans* 'lilac/blue') showing flowers, and the *Teucrium × lucidrys* in the knot garden still in bloom. Strong yellows are represented by the perennial Compositae, *Rudbeckia fulgida* var. *sullivantii* 'Goldsturm' and heliopsis, and the annual *R.* 'Marmalade'. Paler yellow *Anthemis tinctoria* 'E. C. Buxton' has been in flower since June; this will become straggly if not dead-headed regularly, with some of the stems cut right down in order to encourage new growth from the base. (These shoots make excellent cuttings.) The clumps of *Sedum spectabile* are still attractive but no longer provide nectar for the peacock and tortoiseshell butterflies.

The *Cyclamen hederifolium* under the evergreen oak began flowering in

*M*any years ago in a Normandy garden I was struck by the beauty of a border designed by Russell Page, filled with cosmos and white dahlias. Now at Barnsley we grow these annual *Cosmos* 'Sensation'. Dead-headed regularly, they flower from July until the first frost. They are wonderful for picking for the house.

On the left the scented evergreen *Osmanthus delavayi* flowers in March and April. A vigorous wisteria enjoys its south-east-facing place on the house, and so does the winter-flowering *Clematis cirrhosa* var. *balearica*.

August before the leaves emerged – in October the flowers are still coming through the prettily marked foliage, and the earliest flowers have formed seed heads at the end of their corkscrew-shaped stems.

At a moment in early November I have to make a decision: do we allow the leaves and stems of the herbaceous plants to die before we cut them down and thus create spaces to plant the tulip bulbs (delivered in October) we are waiting anxiously to get into the soil? This is a dilemma I have brought on myself – we must 'plant in layers', so that through the seasons there will be a continuity of colour from spring to autumn.

I believe it is important to do as much dividing of perennials as possible in autumn, when the soil is still warm, and to put in new plants so they become established before winter frost sets in, then they will be ready to grow away quickly when spring comes. We treat the salvias, penstemons and diascias as half-hardies, and dig and pot them to overwinter in our polytunnel. Their place is then filled with hundreds of tulips. First forget-me-nots are planted 20–25 cm (8–10 in) apart, and then the tulips are added between them. The forget-me-nots always reseed themselves and we leave enough of these in out-of-the-way corners to grow on and be ready for replanting with the tulips. We sow nigella in 'plugs' in August, and these will be small but sturdy plants by November.

I cannot resist ordering a few small narcissus each year, and I like to put these in groups of thirty or so along the front of the borders. The *Iris reticulata* and species crocus go on the corners of the beds, ready to enjoy in early spring. The mixed borders are all full of narcissus and white Dutch crocus, which we leave in but add more crocus every year, to flower in February or March. The small field mice must have an acute sense of smell, for they arrive and leave a tell-tale hole where they have had a meal. We put mouse traps baited with peanut butter and every morning after planting the crocus there is always a catch to reduce their population.

Not many shrubs are autumn-flowering – berries are more abundant – but we have one speciality: the evergreen *Itea ilicifolia*, now well-established on a north-west-facing wall. The itea, a shrub from the United States, has holly-like leaves, bright glossy green with spiny teeth. At a distance the greenish-white, pendulous flowers could well be mistaken for those of garrya. They are sweetly scented, especially when picked and taken indoors, and appear first in August. They gradually grow longer, and by October are still most impressive.

The Himalayan honeysuckle, *Leycesteria formosa*, is another favourite for autumn attraction. It is deciduous and has hollow, sea-green stems. By rights it should be in the 'Summer' chapter, for its white flowers in dense drooping panicles first appear in June, each small flower surrounded by claret-coloured bracts. By September these have become berries, matching the bracts in colour and making a very distinctive effect. Hollow stems are

Successful planting often happens by chance. Here the clipped pyramid box, the *Euonymus alatus* and the Irish junipers, all united by the ribbon beds, were planted at different times. The four junipers were the first feature, then we planted the box edging and the euonymus, and finally the pyramid box were added as a full stop. In October the standard euonymus (spindle) become a fiery red.

The tall junipers echo the pillars of the temple. This photograph shows the variegated ivy, *Hedera colchica* 'Sulphur Heart', through which we grow *Rosa* 'Golden Showers' and *Clematis* 'Jackmanii' – a purple and gold theme.

impossible to root from cuttings, so we are lucky that the birds enjoy the berries (its other common name is the 'pheasant shrub'). We have three well-established specimens and now find volunteer seedlings throughout the garden where birds, probably the blackbirds – pheasants don't come into the garden – have enjoyed the berries and deposited the seed via their droppings.

Peggy Münster, who created a famous garden at Bampton Manor in Oxfordshire, sowed the seed of many original gardening thoughts in my mind, about both design and the use of plants. She gave me cuttings of an ivy she had growing along the base of a wall, a form of *Hedera colchica*, the Persian ivy, and now we have this as a feature under a lime tree which has a low wall around its trunk. At Wisley I saw *H. c.* 'Arborescens' as a rounded bush; now, twenty years on, ours is a dome 2 metres (6 ft) tall and 3 metres

(10 ft) wide, and in September when the flowers open it is abuzz with any insects which are about collecting nectar. These flowers will soon become black fruit, staying through the winter. Dense ivy is an important hiding-place for tits and sparrows on stormy and freezing days.

Every day there are changes. Some leaves die sadly, others with flamboyance. It is essential to 'catch the moment'. Out of my window I have a panoramic view of 'the wilderness'. Planted since 1960, this has several moments of beauty through the year – daffodils, blossom, summer shade. In summer it can take care of itself, but in autumn it is exciting to stroll there as often as I can, to notice and enjoy the moment when the colouring of the leaves is dominant and the fruits and berries merge in.

Thirty-five years ago I was advised to plant trees and shrubs which thrive on oolitic limestone soil – to forget about rhododendrons, azaleas, and follow the dictates of our natural trees, crataegus, mountain ash, oak, beech. For our garden we chose sorbus, prunus and malus, and an amelanchier. This has paid off, and now every autumn we also have a touch of gold from the ginkgos, which drop their leaves almost overnight. The amelanchier should be tucked away, for its flowering time and best autumn colour last only brief moments. Plant hundreds of blue scillas under *A. canadensis* to coincide with the white/pink blossom.

There are three crab apples: *Malus toringoïdes* with jewel-like yellow berries, *M. transitoria*, whose red fruits are never stolen by the birds, and the popular *M.* 'Golden Hornet', always so full of fruit that the branches are weighed down.

Fruits and autumn-colouring leaves have appeared on the species of mountain ash which love our alkaline soil – *Sorbus cashmiriana* with large white berries silhouetted against the blue autumn sky, and *S.* 'Joseph Rock' with smaller, yellow fruits. (I have planted this tree beside *S. sargentiana*, as Joseph Rock was a plant hunter sent by Charles Sprague Sargent to collect trees and shrubs from China for the Arnold Arboretum in Boston.) In mid-November 'Joseph Rock' still has a hazy canopy of yellow berries, but the birds have already taken every vestige of the thousands of red berries from *S. sargentiana*.

Other star turns are *S.* 'Embley', outstanding with clusters of small red berries and leaves turning a brilliant crimson, and *S. hupehensis*, always prolific with its white-becoming-pink fruits. The pale pink berries of *S. vilmorinii* are highlighted in front of *Parrotia persica*. The parrotia leaves hung on much longer in 1995 – was it because they nearly dropped them during the September drought and then, revitalized by October rain, made the most of the Indian summer? They seemed to decide to hang on as long as possible, and give generously of their best, on into November. Look closely at the parrotia branches, and you can already see the small black buds which will open to become the beautiful but inconspicuous flowers of February.

*V*istas are important in a garden, whatever its size, and it is exciting to create them. This view towards the Gothick summer-house is one of my favourites. On the right, the *Rosa rugosa* hedge is dying from honey fungus, so we are planning a display of bright dahlias, marigolds and nasturtiums for late summer.

On the left the holly, clipped into four tiers, has a beech and yew hedge to lead your eye to the focal point. Since this picture was taken, we have cut off the lower branches of the *Quercus ilex* to reveal the top of the summer-house. This shows the importance of a constant review of the garden, looked at with a critical eye. The yellow shrub on the left is *Ligustrum ovalifolium* 'Aureum', and above this is *Cotinus coggygria* 'Foliis Purpureis'.

Hidden away is an important surprise: by October and November *Euonymus alatus* will have taken on a dazzling colour change – turn the corner, and you will see this spindle as a wonderful shrub, essential for autumn. Other excitements for me are the turning leaves on the mulberry and the ginkgo, both becoming a rich chartreuse-yellow as they fall. In our long border the *Gleditsia triacanthos* 'Sunburst' and the elm *Ulmus minor* 'Dampieri Aurea' become more intensely golden.

The leaves of *Cotinus coggygria* 'Royal Purple' and *C. c.* 'Notcutt's Variety' are dramatic. Next to them the leaves have fallen from *Cornus mas*, but buds are already swelling along the branches for next year's February flowers. The leaves on the deciduous *Metasequoia glyptostroboïdes* are changing to golden before they fall, the *Catalpa bignonioïdes* has dropped all its large leaves, and so has the tulip tree, but these are lying in an alluring pool around their trunks.

At Barnsley we are lucky to have many mature trees – planes, chestnuts, limes, acacias, oaks and beech – planted in the nineteenth century as windbreaks and to line the drive, and also those we have added since 1960.

They give much-needed protection from the west and the north winds, but they also involve a lot of work as they lose their leaves. Each year is different. When it is dry, they can be gathered up easily by raking, and using our efficient Billy Goat (like an industrial hoover), helped by the wind blowing them against the wall, ready to be gathered. Other years, leaf-fall will coincide with rain and the leaves will drop wet and bedraggled, to lie on the lawn by the front drive and cover the path under the lime and laburnum walk and the walnut tree. They must be cleared almost daily, or the worms will drag them down into the lawn and cars travelling up the drive will flatten them, making them doubly difficult to sweep up – when they are like this, the Billy Goat cannot cope with them.

At this time of year the sun is always low in the sky. It can blind us with its brilliance and then play tricks, lighting up features we hardly notice on summer days. It could be the light on an east-facing wall that catches my attention, or a pyracantha still full of berries, or the sunlight illuminating the purple leaves and the fuzz of a cotinus.

These are special moments to remember – highlights which occur when the sun is south of the equator. The newly gilded weathercock on our church tower glistens against the blue evening sky; it has become a background feature in our garden scene. The air is sharp, and we can enjoy all our five senses. The scent of the dying walnut leaves and of the ivy flowers is strong upon the air. The ivy attracts insects, bees, wasps and hover flies, and the box has its own autumn scent, and so does the soil. It is all there for us to appreciate, but one day the scent is here, the next day it has gone.

On early November days, as I look out of my bedroom window while I'm dressing, and the rising sun highlights the transient, ever-changing garden foliage, I can see across the main borders and into the wilderness. In the border the leaves on the red-stemmed dogwood, *Cornus alba* 'Sibirica', are turning gold and crimson, and below is a pool of hosta leaves, once grey and now buttercup-yellow. Nick my gardener and I decide they can stay for a few more days as an extra fillip before they finally lose their beauty. Then they will be relegated to the compost heap – nature re-cycling itself.

*A*n unusual view of the south-east and south-west façades of the house, seen through the framework of an iron seat marketed by my son Charles. The south-west façade has had many changes. Windows were removed on the first floor (you can see their original outlines) when William Pitt set a tax on windows in the eighteenth century. My late husband David put in the ogee-arched window from a demolished house in Cheltenham.

The veranda was added in the 1830s, and an old photograph shows it completely covered with Virginia creeper.

The cyclamen, *C. hederifolium* spp., growing around the trunk of the *Quercus ilex* are seedlings from my original planting made in 1969/1970. I had received a windfall cheque for £10 from *Country Life* for an article I had sent them – and that's how my writing began. A vista takes your eye towards the archway into our plant sales area.

BENINGTON LORDSHIP

Sarah Bott and her husband Harry love the park and garden at all times of the year. Maybe some autumn evenings they find time to sit on the veranda built by Harry's grandparents and watch the setting sun lighten the leaves on the shrubs and trees as they start to turn colour. Sarah has thought much about the joy of the garden in autumn, planting both for berries and for foliage effect.

This view from the veranda, looking over the two ponds Sarah has cleverly incorporated into the garden, changes through the seasons. In summer it is a harmony of green shapes; in winter the bare stems of the willows and dogwoods are red and golden, reflected in the water. In autumn the scene is different again.

The sorbus, which do well on a neutral-to-alkaline soil, are important. In 1979 the National Gardens Scheme gave the Botts a specimen *Sorbus commixta* 'Embley', in recognition of the fact that the garden had been open for fifty years, ever since the scheme started – a wonderful achievement. This sorbus has spectacular autumn colour and a wealth of bright red berries, which the birds take as soon as they ripen. Nearby is *S. hupehensis*, whose blue-grey leaves colour well and then as they fall in October reveal a wealth of white-tinged pink fruits. As well as looking at these from the veranda and the terraces, it is worth walking around the pond and pausing under the trees.

Two special 'thorns' are featured in the garden, *Crataegus prunifolia* and *C. × grignonensis*. *Malus × robusta* 'Red Sentinel' is a favourite of Sarah, but luckily not of the birds, and has a place in many areas of the garden. It looks spectacular in autumn and into winter. Any of these would be a good choice for the small garden where an autumn feature is wanted. If there is space enough, a dramatic background tree which turns a spectacular gold in autumn is the weeping lime, *Tilia petiolaris*. I love the dramatic way the

Looking across the main pond which Sarah has incorporated into the garden, in the evening light. The large leaves of the *Gunnera manicata* contrast with the leaves of *Prunus serrula* on the right and the silver birch across the water. The square tower of the Norman church can be seen now that many of the autumn leaves have fallen. Standing on a gentle rise, it is a reminder of the antiquity of this place.

145

ancient *Ginkgo biloba*, 'the maidenhair tree', sheds its leaves. Having turned a vibrant yellow, on one day these will all fall together, as though a gust of wind had caught them. If you stand still you can hear them rustle, and then a golden carpet spreads round the trunk.

Sarah has not forgotten the value of rose hips; she has planted Rose 'Geranium' (a garden form of *R. moyesii*) all around the urn on the terrace

LEFT *I*n October the garden takes on an autumnal role. Winding paths lead you round, then down to the ponds, so you can admire at close quarters the shrubs Sarah has chosen for their berries, fruits and colouring leaves. She likes the relaxed look, as though it has all happened naturally. Here the flowering crab *Malus × robusta*, commonly known as 'Red Sentinel', overhangs the path. These red fruits are cherry-like and have no calyxes. The spring blossom is pink/white.

In the background you see the wing and top of the veranda added by Harry Bott's grandparents in 1906. Although built in keeping with the architecture of the eighteenth-century house, it spoils the Georgian symmetry.

BELOW *H*ere at Benington Lordship, autumn is as colourful and well considered as every other season. On the wall behind one perennial border *Solanum jasminoides* 'Album' has woven its way through Virginia creeper (*Vitis quinquefolia*). The pure white flowers of the potato vine make the vivid red leaves vibrate – but only for a few days, and when they fall there will be a crimson pool beneath.

Some of the shrubs were planted by Sarah's in-laws, but she has greatly extended the repertoire to include her own favourites, and has used every opportunity to cover any space available.

below the rose garden. In September and October the wall backing the herbaceous border becomes alive with white *Solanum jasminoides* 'Album', flowering beside and through Virginia creeper as this turns a fiery red. Some autumn bulbs have established and increased, especially sternbergia and nerines under south-facing walls, but the *Galtonia candicans* may need replenishing each year. So with careful thought every month has its interest.

WINTER

We must never think of the garden as dying in December, it is just resting to gain vigour for next year. We can only see what is happening above ground but roots are still active and worms are working below. We enjoy the shapes of our shrubs, some with vividly coloured stems, the silhouettes of the deciduous trees and the impact of the evergreens and any berries which the birds have left. It is fun to make a list of flowers in bloom on Boxing Day.

Any plants which have winter or Christmas in their common name should be flowering: winter jasmine, winter honeysuckle, wintersweet. *Viburnum fragrans*, the name telling us that like many other winter flowers its are scented, is ready to pick and bring indoors.

Hellebores are my best stand-by. *Helleborus niger*, the Christmas rose, comes out first and then *H. foetidus* display their lime-green flowers before the *H. orientalis* open. Other excitements come when the winter aconites, the first crocus and *Iris reticulata* open. They are all part of our late winter glory.

The garden at Bledlow Manor has Robert Adams' formal structure enhanced by Lady Carrington's planting and Lord Carrington's imagination. The narrow arch in the yew hedge leads from the rose garden, the first of the architectural spaces, into the St Peter garden (see page 80). Many of the roses have been replaced by evergreen and shapely shrubs to provide both summer and winter interest.

Frost picks up the outlines and veining of the evergreen senecio and *Viburnum davidii*, the rounded shape of lavender in the foreground, and the upright stems of rosemary on the left. The unseen central beds in this garden are still filled with roses, those Iona has chosen as best to pick for the house.

BLEDLOW MANOR

My walk with Peter Carrington in the garden at Bledlow in winter took us through the formal, architectural parts of the garden – the rose garden, and then through an archway in the yew hedge into St Peter's garden. To complete the trio, you walk on into the armillary garden. In winter these all look crisp and comfortable. It is the design which is important. Peter expressed it, 'One bit of a garden should connect to the next, not be separate rooms.' Yew hedges become important in winter and, as he remarked, 'I don't think they look right if they are untidy.'

Rose gardens are dull and dead-looking in winter unless other shrubs are included. Here at Bledlow the roses are confined to the central beds while the surrounding borders are filled with evergreen and grey-leaved shrubs. They give shape and structure and on frosty days have a special quality in contrast to their background of dark yew.

Leaving these three architectural gardens, you walk along the north-facing side of the manor, where Iona has planted enough evergreen and grey shrubs immediately under the house walls to make you aware that a garden can have interest in winter.

The ground slopes towards the long ornamental pool, and on the way the beds are built up with brick surrounds, as though they were shallow terraces. Beyond the pool, through a gate and over the old farm road, is Peter's sculpture garden, described in more detail in the 'Autumn' chapter. In winter, when the deciduous trees and shrubs are bare, there is an embracing view towards Bledlow church.

This encouraged me to go over the village road into the Lyde Garden – I wanted to see it before the spring leaf buds opened, while the trees were still sculptured skeletons reflected in the three pools. As we negotiated the steps down to the bottom of the ravine, the eleventh-century church loomed high above us on our left, poised serenely only 3 metres (10 ft) away from the cliff edge. The scene was dramatic, and so was my host – a great raconteur – who declaimed in a forceful, rustic voice an old local saying: 'Those who live and do abide shall see Bledlow church fall in the Lyde.' The Carringtons have done what they could in this century to stabilize the steep bank, by planting trees and shrubs to hold the soil.

The reflections of the trees were crystal clear, and as I stood on the bridge where the willow overhangs I could see the eye-catcher bought by the Carringtons at Christie's – a small aviary which dominates the upper pond, giving an oriental touch to this English garden.

$\mathcal{T}$o find the Lyde valley, you must leave the main garden and cross the village road. Made in a deep ravine created by springs tipping for years into the small River Lyde, it has a wonderful atmosphere of mystery, especially on wintry days.

After elm disease had struck, leaving a wilderness of brambles, elder and ash saplings, the Carringtons decided to make a secret garden, which the whole village could walk and sit in and enjoy. Robert Adams helped design three connecting pools with a continuous surrounding path and a simple rustic bridge and walkway made from Ghanaian hardwood. The planting has grown to be lush and natural-looking. This willow, with its roots in a moist spot, frames the small white aviary set in the middle of the upper pond; it gives the garden a slightly Japanese look.

$\mathcal{A}$ brick path leads you from the rose garden, through the St Peter garden into the most architectural of the compartments designed by Robert Adams, all enclosed with yew hedges. The centrepiece, an armillary sphere set on a handsome pillar, is surrounded by clipped box. Four solid cubes topped by impressive balls echo the shape of the intricate sphere. The tops of the simple geometric shapes are clearly defined by the gentle fall of snow.

This is a cool garden to walk through before you reach the borders by the house, the long ornamental pool and Iona's herbaceous borders.

THE GROVE

A fine winter day – preferably with snow on the ground – shows off the structure of the garden at The Grove to perfection. In a blue sky patterned with billowing clouds the sun, always low in late winter, makes the snow sparkle, and casts sharp shadows.

To understand the plan of the 1.6 hectare (4 acre) garden you must first stand, as David Hicks did in 1980, looking from the windows of the four main rooms of the house: the living room, dining room, library and the main bedroom. From the living room you look out to the south. Twelve box-edged rectangles decorate a flat mown lawn; the level then rises, steeply at first, then more gently. Here David, a master of scale and architectural structure, has created a striking vista. Remember his philosophy that interior and exterior must be linked. The grass vista is the width of the living room with a central mown lawn, and on each side are strips of longer grass, cut once a year. The 'walls' of this vista are pleached hornbeams on 1.35 metre (4½ ft) trunks, and beneath and slightly behind these is a hedge, also of hornbeam. This gives a feeling of solidity, but also of rhythm, created by the regularity of the hornbeam trunks, 1.2 metres (4 ft) apart. The gardeners, Paul Ballard and Peter Church, tell me they keep

This view from the main living room on the south side of the house demonstrates David's love of symmetry. In winter it is a panorama of simple geometric shapes, using straight lines with squares and rectangles. The gentle rise gives a feeling of depth and opens up the vista. It is a linear design on a grand scale.

In summer this view is a symphony of green on green – the walls of the two 'rooms' are solid – but in winter you can see through the tracery of the hornbeams. David brought the ornamental urns on pedestals, which mark the corners of the hedges, from their family home at Britwell.

OVERLEAF *T*he swimming pool is a visual delight in winter. The central feature looking from the dining room to the west side of the house, it is framed by standard horse chestnut trees, underplanted with a hedge of the same species. Urns on pedestals mark the corners of this garden room.

David's attention to detail is illustrated here by the surround of the pool – first with a stone rim, then a strip of cobbles and finally the grass. These three textures retain their interest through the year. An avenue of horse chestnuts extends into the distance as far as the eye can see, which on this misty winter day is left to the imagination.

every hedge in trim using hand clippers. Electric clippers are not allowed, and this brings home to me the precision demanded and achieved – no leaves and stems are spoilt, for the human hand and human eye are working in harmony.

The scale is perfect, and the rising ground helps to make the structure of this vista more apparent. Beyond the hornbeam, a central gate in a see-through wooden fence with slim uprights veils the termination of the vista. The fence is framed at each end by brick piers topped with pinnacles made of marine plywood. As the ground is still rising, the 'Gothic tent' can be seen and becomes the focal point at the end of the straight grass path. David devised this tent using hornbeams trained up and over an iron framework made for him by the local blacksmith. Looking out from it, you find that the vista continues across the next field with an avenue of Spanish sweet chestnuts, *Castanea sativa*, 400 metres (¼ mile) long.

The view to the west from the dining-room window was planned at the same time as the view from the living room. Here there is another very architectural concept, different but equally satisfying. You step out on to a stone paved terrace and down two steps towards a rectangular swimming

A winter view of the red garden, also shown in summer leaf on page 90. This is a small, square 'room' you pass through rather than sit in as you stroll in the garden.

The limestone urn is set in an alcove of copper beech and four wooden obelisks create a structure for the winter when the rose stems are bare. Notice the crenellations over the concealed gate on the right which leads you into the main lawn in front of the house.

When beech is trimmed as a hedge or topiary, it retains its juvenile form, keeping its leaves through the winter, unlike a mature beech tree, which loses all its leaves in late autumn.

pool set at right angles to the house. The inside of the pool is painted black, so that it looks like a stretch of formal water rather than a swimming pool, and constantly mirrors the sky. In every part of the garden you notice David's meticulous attention to detail, and here the pool is surrounded with regular-sized rectangular stone slabs, surrounded in their turn by a band, 40.5 cm (16 in) wide, of cobblestones set in cement. This immediately presents four different textures: water, stone, pebbles and lawn.

On three sides of this swimming-pool garden – a perfect extension of the dining room – are horse chestnuts, *Aesculus hippocastanum*. Again David has planted standard trees combined with a hedge; the chestnuts are on 2 metre (6 ft) trunks and 1.5 metres (5 ft) apart, with a chestnut hedge between them. Now sixteen years old, both trees and hedges are hard-clipped each spring, and have now reached their destined height. In summer the large leaves make a solid curtain, and in winter when the slanting sun is shining the bare branches trace shadows on the red-brick wall of the old barn some 2 metres (6 ft) behind. In the farthest corners of this living rectangular 'room' are two urns on pedestals.

David has extended the vista beyond the pool 'room' by planting an avenue of horse chestnuts 530 metres (⅓ mile) long, and persuading the neighbouring landowner to allow him to cut a narrow *clairvoyée* through a stand of trees on the horizon, thus bringing the landscape into the garden. On windy days the chestnut leaves move and rustle, and even on a still day there is the intermittent movement of field birds flying across the avenue – partridge, pigeons, rooks, and a red kite with a huge wingspan. Every day as you look along the avenue the rabbits and birds are busy.

The east view from the library and the main bedroom is different. You see the approach to the house and the drive comes in at an angle, mostly hidden by a large holly tree, but David has cut an *oeil-de-boeuf* through this, just large enough and so positioned that, standing at the front door, he can see whether the steel gate is shut on the drive.

The rule of no colour near the house is broken here, with drifts of narcissus and crocus in spring. But David's sense of symmetry and eye for detail are apparent in the two large metal dogs guarding the door, and two square wooden tubs painted a subtle grey-beige containing carefully clipped standard crataegus with beech, kept to only 40.5 cm (16 in) high, under and round them.

In 1993 14,000 young hardwoods were planted in the land just beyond the garden, to make a windbreak in a few decades' time and in February 1995 his two stalwart gardeners Paul and Peter were making another long vista a quarter of a mile from the house, through a stand of re-growth elms. From the front door you will be able to see through this vista and beyond to the Chiltern hills 8 km (5 miles) away. David's ideas are unending.

*T*he strong patterns in the green garden make it as interesting in winter as it is in summer. It is enclosed by stone walls and stilt hornbeams, with a hornbeam hedge behind. The drawbridge, operated electrically by pressing a button, lowers itself over the canal and leads to the pavilion.

The large pots are plastic and emerge from a rectangular platform of hawthorn clipped to the height of the pots. In this picture the potted mulberries have now been exchanged for artichokes and in the adjacent rectangle are more artichokes, dramatic in summer. The effective cubist acorn on top of the stone pillar is a typical example of David's design detail.

KIFTSGATE COURT

Anne is enthusiastic about the garden in winter. As you stand on the edge of the steep bank looking through the pine trees, on clear days there is a perfect view across the vale to the Malvern Hills. The bank faces west, so the setting sun adds its own colour to the trees and the sky. It is in these winter months that you can appreciate the beauty of the pines with their underplanting of evergreens, berberis, bergenias, ceanothus, hollies and hypericums, and the sword-leaves of phormiums and yuccas.

In the garden near the house, Anne says: 'Our best winter tree is *Prunus incisa* 'Praecox', flowering from December to January' – the pink buds open to white blossom. It is a form of the Fuji cherry, a Japanese species long used for bonsai; this species received an Award of Merit from the Royal Horticultural Society in 1957: like Sarah Bott at Benington Lordship, Anne appreciates the importance of winter flowers for their scent. Among the interesting trees and shrubs planted in the small arboretum along the drive is an established *Magnolia campbellii mollicomata* which opens its large pink to rose-purple flowers in February.

In the white sunk garden there is a well-grown *Hamamelis mollis*, the most popular of the Chinese witch hazels. Reliable and very fragrant, the golden yellow flowers last from December through to February. Some of the viburnums have frost-hardy flowers and, carefully chosen, can scent parts of the garden all winter. At Kiftsgate there are *Viburnum* × *bodnantense*, which produces its flowers as early as November and continues throughout the winter, and *V. burkwoodii*, an evergreen which blooms from January until May.

From Christmas until spring all through the garden hellebores, snow-drops and winter aconites open in great carpets. There are banks of them up the drive and in the bluebell wood. Snowdrops can be increased by digging and dividing them 'in the green' in February, and winter aconites are easily increased by collecting the seed as soon as it ripens and scattering it about. They grow well under deciduous trees and shrubs and look especially good mixed with snowdrops.

Every season has its own beauty. Simon Verity's seat, commissioned by Diany in 1976, has a backing of beech hedge and today has a white, snow-apron. Pause and enjoy her form and movement on a winter day. She is framed by an arch of *Sorbus aria* 'Lutescens', trained and clipped to cover the wide arch.

Both Stephen Crisp, the present head gardener, and his predecessor Mr Hatton, who started work here in 1962, have planted with winter interest in mind. Mrs Hatton took care of the flower arrangements throughout the house, and as a background for exotic winter flowers (mostly from her husband's greenhouses) she liked to use leaves in a variety of textures, elaeagnus, hebes and senecio, box and skimmia – this often has a supply of red berries, as well as evergreen leaves. Mrs Hatton remembers how Mrs Bruce, wife of Ambassador David Bruce (1961–69), sometimes liked to have her dining-room tables decorated with arrangements of vegetables, chosen for their colour, texture and shape.

Among Stephen's talents is his skill in flower arranging, and he is now responsible for decorating the house. In the large reception rooms, displays must be in proportion to the grandeur of the architecture, but he also delights in creating tiny bouquets for breakfast trays, and bedroom posies. His artistic eye takes him unerringly to the leaves which match and complement individual flowers, and to colours which blend with the room they are to enhance.

The responsibility of the head gardener at Winfield House is different from that of the usual head gardener, who works for a permanent boss. The ambassador in residence is likely to move on after four or five years, so Stephen feels that his main responsibility is towards the garden. He has a free hand, though he always refers to the ambassador before any major change or expenditure.

Talking with Stephen, I was much impressed by the financial savings he is able to make for the embassy, especially considering London prices, by using home-grown flowers, evergreens, and plants from the greenhouse. The same shrubs make an essential contribution in the garden in winter. The ever-greys have their charm and lighten the effect in the borders on 'crisp', often cloudless days, when the sun will highlight textures and colours.

The twelve *Magnolia grandiflora*, planted in 1992 boldly against the north-facing wall of the house and now 4 metres (13 ft) tall, give year-long interest to the approach to the front door, providing a formal structure, with their large dramatic polished leaves shiny green on top and reddish-brown underneath. Two more in Versailles planters stand each side of the front door to give a feeling of welcome. The highly scented, creamy-white flowers open from June onwards, through the summer. Small flowers like those of *Spiraea* 'Arguta' need to blossom in sprays or clusters to make an impact while others, like the luscious *Magnolia grandiflora*, can open individually, each bloom demanding attention. It is sad that sometimes we are deterred from planting a beautiful shrub because we know it will be seven years or more before it will flower. This magnolia is one such, but a knowledgeable nursery may advise you to choose *M. g.* 'Exmouth', or

On a wintry day Barbara Hutton's beautiful figure still sits silently, looking on to the leafless trees surrounding the green lawn and the distant water. Her profile contrasts with the tracery of the trees and the Post Office Tower. Pebbles introduce both movement and design, and act as a foil to the surrounding boxwood and the brickwork. Notice the billowing clouds above the London sky.

you can search for and plant a mature specimen. You do not need a grand Georgian house; a barn wall or a gable end will suffice.

Viburnums are essential shrubs in the garden in winter, some for their evergreen leaves, others for flowers and scent. At Winfield Stephen has planted groups of the tall *Viburnum rhytidophyllum* – they have large, rather corrugated leaves which create a wonderful sound-barrier against traffic. You need one male bush among the females to get a good crop of fruits. Quite different in texture, structure and shape is *V. davidii*, useful for another reason: I think of it as a ground-cover shrub, making a symmetrical mound about 70 cm (2 ft) in height. The evergreen leaves are a dark, glossy green, with unscented white flowers in June, but if luck is on your side there will be a harvest of bright, turquoise blue berries through the winter. This virburnum, too, is grown at Winfield House.

Much the same mounded shape as *V. davidii* is the evergreen *Skimmia japonica*, and again you must have one male among your female plants in order to get a crop of red berries, which will persist all winter. Unless you have a very reliable nurseryman, my advice is to buy container-grown plants in April or May when they are in flower, then you can be sure to select one male to two or more females: it is disappointing to discover after several years that you only have male plants, which never provide you with berries. *Skimmia reevesiana* is a species on which the flowers are bisexual but I have found it to be disappointing. It will produce berries, but not in enough quantity to be satisfactory and eye-catching.

*T*he short drive takes you from the Inner Circle of Regent's Park through the iron entrance gates. From the sound and the constant movement of the traffic you enter the curving drive to approach the handsome brick façade with its portico and Tuscan columns. Evergreen shrubs on the right and left balance the proportions of the house, and with the line of twelve *Magnolia grandiflora* on this north-west-facing façade you can appreciate the careful thought that has gone into making Winfield a mature country garden in the heart of London.

The scented-flowered viburnums in the garden include *Viburnum farreri, V. × bodnantense* and *V. carlesii*. Stephen has planted elaeagnus for evergreen leaves and autumn scent. With their strong growth they are useful for picking for winter arrangements, as is the winter-flowering evergreen *Viburnum tinus*.

We must not forget to walk in the rose garden in winter. We all agree that stems of rose bushes after pruning look like unattractive bare legs, so Sir Peter Shepherd, who designed this garden in 1983 for Ambassador and Mrs John Louis, enclosed it with a yew hedge. The paths are of two contrasting textures, York stone and squares of grass, and all the beds are edged with *Bergenia cordifolia* and nepeta, with accents of lavender and santolina.

The central feature in this garden is a dome-shaped arbour covered by two *Rosa* 'The Garland' and two *R. banksiae* 'Lutea Plena'. These ramblers flower in sequence, the later being 'The Garland'. Stephen has to take them down every two years for a major pruning, during winter, and the job takes two people three days by the time they have re-tied the stems and cleared away all the clippings.

Down by the lake there are plantings of dogwoods – *Cornus alba* 'Sibirica', the Westonbirt dogwood with brilliant crimson shoots, and the golden-stemmed form, *C. a.* 'Spaethii' – and willows are also well represented. *Salix alba vitellina* 'Britzensis' has striking orange-scarlet branches, and there is the form with vivid yellow branches. Catkins are important, both in the garden and for February arrangements in the house, and *S. daphnoïdes* is one of the best. The purple-violet shoots have a white bloom, and then the catkins, also with a purple haze, develop early in the year and are loved by the bees for their early pollen. Stephen 'stools' these dogwoods and willows just before the sap starts to rise each spring, to allow the new shoots a full season of growth.

It is rewarding to take a leisurely early spring walk round the lake before the leaves open on the trees. The underplanting has drifts of hellebores, *H. orientalis, H. foetidus* and *H. argutifolius* (until recently known as *H. corsicus*).

Among the happy memories Mrs Crowe will one day take home with her from her years in England will undoubtedly be the trees. 'I think they are fantastic. Some are so huge you just can't get your arms around them. I appreciate them much more, I think, than I do the flowers.' Looking at his wife, Admiral Crowe said affectionately, 'Shirley has a passion for trees.' She responded thoughtfully: 'Of course, in Oklahoma trees are precious. You learn to appreciate a tree, because we don't have a lot of them.' 'It's a great plain state, very flat, with corn and wheat,' added the ambassador.

Here in the heart of London is a garden with both trees and flowers, a garden for all seasons, planted as a country garden with the advantage of a city microclimate.

Winter is the time when you can stand back and see the different winter pictures. These can be patterns we ourselves have made, or patterns made by the shapes of evergreens and the silhouettes of deciduous trees.

The structure of paths, steps, hedges, arbours and walls becomes important when the perennial plants are below ground. Our eighteenth-century stone wall is most alive in summer, but through the winter months I love to work on it, pruning back and tying in the branches of the roses, weaving in the honeysuckle and clematis stems. Many years ago we secured old 10 cm (4 in) pig netting to the wall; this is virtually invisible and saves time in adding extra nails.

The evergreens stand out. There is *Itea ilicifolia*, *Hedera colchica* 'Sulphur Heart', a variegated cotoneaster and a *Mahonia japonica*. Under all these we watch the *Helleborus orientalis* slowly developing for their display. Gradually we cut off the leaves to allow the flower stems to show in their full glory. These plants, originally from Nancy Lindsay, have been here many years and now range in colour from pure to speckled white, through pink to darkest claret. By February their seedlings will be coming through.

My stone gardeners guard the iron gate in the wall. Carved from Bath stone by Simon Verity in 1982 and given to David as a birthday present, they are now well weathered, with moss round their hats, boots and cornucopias of flowers and fruits.

Patterns stand out clearly in winter. Our two knots are designs from old books. One is taken from the 1616 English translation by Gervase Markham of a French book; the other, from Stephen Blake's *The Compleat Gardeners Practice*, he calls the true lovers' knot. The box threads of these knots all interlace, and we have clipped them to appear as though they go over and under each other. To be historically correct, the spaces between should be filled with coloured earth in the five heraldic colours: red (broken bricks), yellow (sand), black (pure coal dust), white (chalk) and blue (coal and chalk mixed). We have simply used a local gravel.

Unlike the two square knot patterns, the herb bed is long and narrow, where five diamond shapes are defined in box and infilled with useful herbs for cooking. In winter the compartments stand out and in summer the herbs are predominant.

Many visitors tell me how much they enjoy the vegetable garden. This was inspired by the writing and the designs of the early seventeenth-century writer and clergyman, William Lawson. Today gardeners realize how much artistic potential there can be in growing fruit and vegetables. William Lawson taught me the importance of narrow beds so that the 'weeder women' could work easily from the paths, and also how incorporating flowers with your vegetables can 'make all your senses swim in pleasure'.

A corner of the knot garden, showing clearly how the threads of the pattern can interlace and give a feeling of movement and rhythm. The knot itself is the picture and the surrounding box becomes the frame. In Tudor times, knots were infilled with coloured earths, all heraldic colours – rouge, bleue, noire, argent and gold. The knot on the right comes from a 1664 book and is called 'The True Lovers' Knot'.

You cannot expect to have a bounty of flowers and vegetables in your garden unless you feed them well, always putting back some of those nutrients they use. Nature provides us with compost and leaf mould, or maybe the local farmer will offer you a load of manure when he is clearing out his cowsheds in spring – this gives an abundance of riches.

There are plenty of compost-making systems and bins advertised in the gardening magazines – but my advice to you is to spend a day at the Henry Doubleday Research Association at Ryton-on-Dunsmore in Warwickshire, where you will discover some secrets of compost-making and the benefits of organic gardening.

Here at Barnsley our system is simple: we have a dozen and more hens working for us. They lay eggs, but what is far more important is that all the weeds, prunings, lawn mowings and kitchen waste are put into their run daily. This keeps them occupied, and while they scratch away and provide nitrogen-rich droppings, they are helping to break down all this waste into rich compost. The level in their run gets higher and higher, and then once a year, using a tractor-driven fork lift, it is taken out and stacked ready to be used as potting compost or spread on the borders. For potting compost it is sieved, then mixed with recycled peat and perlite.

The breaking down of the leaf mould is just as exciting. Through October, November and into December the fallen leaves are raked and gathered into a 2.7 metre (2½ yd) square enclosure at the bottom of the drive. As the leaves decompose they quickly heat up.

Then one February or March day, before the spring gardening rush is upon us, the gardeners turn the pile, and by the following autumn it will have become – in just one year – an enviable leaf mould all ready to spread like a beautiful blanket on the borders, feeding them and giving back what has been taken out. This is the cycle of nature.

*T*he winter aconites up the drive are the first important feature in the garden each year, appearing any time between late January and early February. Sometimes when there is snow on the ground they will push through, and as they do so generate enough heat to melt a circle of snow, allowing their buds to be seen. It is always an exciting moment. To increase the aconites, we gather seed immediately it is ripe in May and scatter it around – or dig them 'in the green'. Dried-up corms planted in autumn are rarely successful. ❧

GREAT DIXTER

Although the garden at Great Dixter is not open to the public between November and March, this does not mean that during these five months there are no flowers, shapes, or colour – far from it.

The yew hedges with their scalloped outlines and the various topiary shapes are dominant and dramatic, especially on sunny days when the light catches them, or when they are capped with snow. Within these hedges are scented shrubs. The evergreen mahonias 'Lionel Fortescue' and 'Buckland', with their handsome leaves, make their own statement through the year. The leaves of deciduous *Lonicera* × *purpusii*, *Chimonanthus praecox*, *Hamamelis mollis* and various viburnums, also scented, are coarse, so plant them where their scent can be appreciated but their foliage will be hidden behind something else, or masked by an annual climber or an autumn-flowering clematis.

The bright yellow winter jasmine, *Jasminum nudiflorum*, never fails throughout December and January. Its lax branches suit large or small bouquets. Hellebores, snowdrops, crocus and *Iris reticulata* grow all through the garden, but Christo admits to finding the winter aconites, *Eranthis hyemalis*, difficult to keep going. There are plenty of berries about, enough to feed the birds and decorate the house.

Christo's natural artistry includes cooking and flower arranging, so he must have plenty of herbs, foliage and flowers to use all through the year in the kitchen and the house. Soon we will be able to read in Christo's book – to be published in 1997 – how he prepares and cooks all the vegetable and salad crops he grows in his garden.

The clever link between house and garden is very apparent in winter. The path from the porch door leads to the front gate, and you have the same vista from the guest bedroom window above. On the south side another door takes you on to the upper terrace (an ideal place to sit on summer evenings), while the windows on this side look out to the old rose garden and the orchard. From the east-side windows there are views of the high garden, and of patterns of yew hedges. The house and garden are in harmony. The garden looks inviting from the house, and the house with all its different roof lines looks beautiful at every angle from the garden.

The earliest flowers growing in the meadow each side of the straight stone path leading to Christo's front door start with the white and the purple species crocus, *C. chrysanthus* 'Snow Bunting' and *C. tommasianus*, mixed with yellow *C. flavus*. On sunny February days these crocuses will open for the bees to visit gathering pollen.

It is important to mow this grass in late autumn so the early flowers are revealed as they come through.

BENINGTON LORDSHIP

*A*s far as I know, Sarah and Harry Bott's garden at Benington Lordship, which incorporates the ruins of a Norman keep and moat and a nineteenth-century mock-ancient gate house, all set in established park-land, has never been the subject of an overall master-plan – since 1905 it has simply evolved, as dictated by the parkland trees, the dry moat, the sloping ground leading down on the west side to the old lakes, and the instinctive wish of successive owners to contribute to the whole while maintaining the atmosphere peculiar to a site with such an historic past. You would not, I think, expect to find topiary, or long vistas; the old shrubberies, the Edwardian-style borders and the walled kitchen garden created by Harry Bott's grandparents, all surely influenced by William Robinson (with a touch of Gertrude Jekyll) and reflecting the style of English country estates early this century, seem entirely in keeping, and Sarah Bott has introduced trees, shrubs and perennials of her own choice.

The garden is open every February for the amazing display of snowdrops – carpets of them, the heralds of spring: we all love a taste of this. Harry's grandparents planted a snowdrop walk on the east and south sides of the house, and these snowdrops have multiplied and spread into the nearby moat. Sarah explains how, when she first came to Benington, she found the moat a jungle of brambles and nettles, with nineteen dying elms. When all these had been finally cleared – with the help of family, weekend guests, a goat, and machinery – light and moisture could once more reach the banks. For years the gardeners had unwittingly been making valuable compost and mulch by tossing into the moat all their rakings, mowings and prunings – which must also have included snowdrop seeds and bulbs, for one February soon after the clearing, carpets of them came through and flowered; now they have spread to make closely knit drifts. Following these in March and April another carpet unfolds: Sarah has added hundreds of golden daffodils and blue *Scilla bithynica*.

*E*arly morning sunlight shines on the dramatic carpet of snowdrops, *Galanthus nivalis*, a spectacular sight on February days. It is thanks to Harry's grandparents, who planted a snowdrop walk on the east and south sides of the house, and to the gardeners who over decades tossed rakings and mowings including snowdrop seeds into the Norman moat.

When Sarah and Harry inherited the property and cleared the ancient moat of dying elms, brambles and nettles, the light was let in and the snowdrops regenerated and flowered. Through the trunks of the trees, the east end of the Norman church reminds us once again of the history of this place.

*A*nother view of the snowdrops. We need to be enticed into the garden in February when snow is on the ground, but the reward can be well worth while when the winter aconites (*Eranthis hyemalis*) push through at the same time as the snowdrops to make a carpet of green, gold and white.

In the background the gatehouse makes a theatrical entrance-way.

On the west-facing slope of the moat an expanding clump of white-stemmed *Rubus cockburnianus* has become established. It looks dramatic lit up by the sun, surrounded by snowdrops and winter aconites piercing through the snow. The snowdrops are all the species *Galanthus nivalis*; their sheer quantity and the extent of their carpet creates the drama.

It is exciting to approach the courtyard through the Pulhamite gate-house. This is a sheltered area where *Rosa banksiae* flowers and other half-hardy shrubs do well. *Fremontodendron californicum* survives most winters (such a fast-growing shrub is easily replaced), and the 'allspice', *Calicanthus occidentalis*, has proved totally hardy here. All these are recollections from Sarah's home in Cornwall. A large *Magnolia* × *soulangeana* planted by Mrs Arthur Bott has survived for eighty years and is the living feature in this enclosed space. Here under the east-facing wall of the house Sarah has more galanthus species and is collecting several different-coloured *Helleborus orientalis*.

Going up a flight of steps flanked by evergreen shrubs and *Cotinus coggygria*, you reach the summer-house let into the ruined curtain wall next to the Norman keep. Inside, a buddha sits quietly in a niche above the tombstone of a Greek slave. The pathway from the summer-house takes you to the famous snowdrop walk, along a line of *Viburnum tinus*. If you look up as you pass by here, you will catch a view of the square Norman church tower framed by the bare tracery of deciduous trees.

Sarah loves winter-flowering trees and shrubs, and on the bank on the south side of the house overlooking the rose garden she has planted a row of six *Prunus subhirtella* 'Autumnalis'. From the rose garden the ground slopes steeply down and some wide steps take you to a gravel path where the original drive came straight below past the west side of the house. There is a wonderful view from here towards the two lakes or, as Sarah calls them, 'the ponds'. They are divided by a bastion, a grass pathway leading to the far side of the top pond – a perfect winter walk, with plenty of active wild life. The banks are now planted with willows and alders for their winter catkins and with groups of red- and yellow-stemmed dogwoods, which show up brilliantly when there is snow. Fruits linger on the crab apples, and berries on the cotoneasters. Two of Sarah's recent acquisitions are the pink-flowered variety of *Prunus padus*, from Hergest Croft in Herefordshire, and *Betula albosinensis* var. *septentrionalis*, which she saw at Rockingham Castle; the Chinese red birch has orange-pink or reddish bark, bloomed with violet-white, which it sheds in shaggy rolls.

On the way up from the lake you pass the orchard. Sadly the apple trees are now old and past their best, but the ground under them is blue in March and April with scillas among the daffodils, in May pink with blossom.

This long incline brings you back to the level of the house, passing the old stables; here there is a line of pleached limes. Their old, gnarled branches

The rose garden in winter. Mrs Arthur Bott, Harry's grandmother, designed this rose garden on the south side of the house, overlooked from the main rooms. To reduce labour and overcome rose sickness, Sarah has grassed over the middle beds. Now the roses are 'Margaret Merril' and 'Radox Bouquet', both highly scented. The raised bank beyond, emphasized by the winter shadows, has a line of six *Prunus subhirtella* 'Autumnalis', with semi-double white flowers in February and March and good autumn colour.

The west façade of the church looks long and low beyond the bare trunks of the beech and sycamore trees.

are a fascinating sight in winter, for years ago selected side branches were grafted from each tree into its neighbour, to make a continuous garland.

I left Benington Lordship with an impression of deep admiration for Sarah Bott. Moving from Cornwall, where the climate is mild and camellias and rhododendrons thrive, to cold Hertfordshire with its heavy clay soil must have been quite a shock and a challenge for her. Although parts of the garden were already laid out, which she admits she was glad of, it had been allowed to sleep peacefully in the hands of her husband's parents and of Jim and Edith Collis, who had both worked here for fifty years and were due to retire.

It needed much restoration, cutting back, and an injection of new ideas. Sarah was fortunate to engage Ian Billot, a great enthusiast as well as a knowledgeable gardener. In 1993 Ian left to become head gardener at Sudeley Castle and Sarah was fortunate to find Richard Webb, another talented gardener, to work with her in this romantic garden. Between them, it has been tamed and transformed, the overgrown shrubberies cleared, and wherever a chance has arisen Sarah has found exactly the right tree or shrub to plant.

Every large garden should have an itinerary – think of Stourhead and Rousham – so bringing the ponds into the boundary of the garden was an inspired idea. Now the garden walk is complete, at all seasons.

*F*rost and a sprinkling of snow create this strong contrast of light and shade. Dark, well-clipped yews stand out against the white grass where shadows play an important role. Looking through the veranda along the pathway to the church, the crenellations on the church tower are silhouetted against the grey sky – full of more snow yet to fall. The pathway is edged with lavender and three shrub roses, *Rosa* 'Frühlingsduft', *R.* 'Agnes' and the incense rose, *R. primula.*

GARDEN PLANS

Barnsley House
Barnsley
Gloucestershire

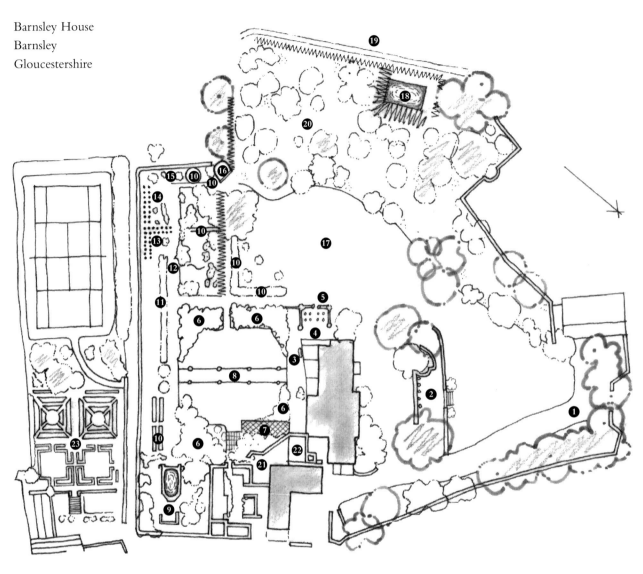

0   10 metres

0   11 yards

1 Drive	13 Laburnum walk
2 Front terrace	14 Winter walk
3 Terrace	15 Frog fountain
4 Veranda	(carved by Simon Verity)
5 Knot garden	16 Gothick summer-house
6 Parterre beds	17 Croquet lawn
7 Herb bed	18 Swimming pool
8 Yew walk	19 Ha-ha
9 Pool garden	20 'The wilderness'
10 Mixed borders	21 Courtyard
11 Lime walk	22 Conservatory
12 Grass walk	23 Potager

Walls

Hedges (yew, beech)

Water

Open all year: Monday, Wednesday,
Thursday, Saturday (10–6).

Benington Lordship
Benington
Hertfordshire

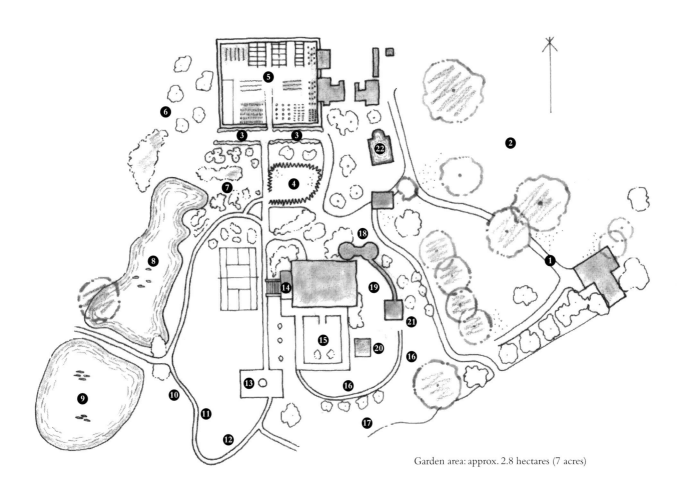

Garden area: approx. 2.8 hectares (7 acres)

 Walls

 Hedges (yew)

Water

Open April through August:
Wednesday 12–5, Sunday 2–5.
September: Wednesday 2–5.
Easter, spring, summer bank holiday
Mondays 12–5.
To see snowdrops telephone 01438 869668
during January for recorded message.

1 Drive
2 Parkland
3 Herbaceous borders
4 Sunk garden
5 Kitchen garden
  and garden centre
6 Orchard
7 Rockery
8 Top pond
9 Lower pond
10 Ha-ha
11 Heather bank

12 Cowslip bank
13 Urn and lawn
14 Veranda
15 Rose garden
16 Snowdrop walk
17 Dry moat
18 Folly
   (neo-Norman gatehouse)
19 Courtyard
20 Norman keep
21 Summer-house
22 Swimming pool

Bledlow Manor
Bledlow
Buckinghamshire

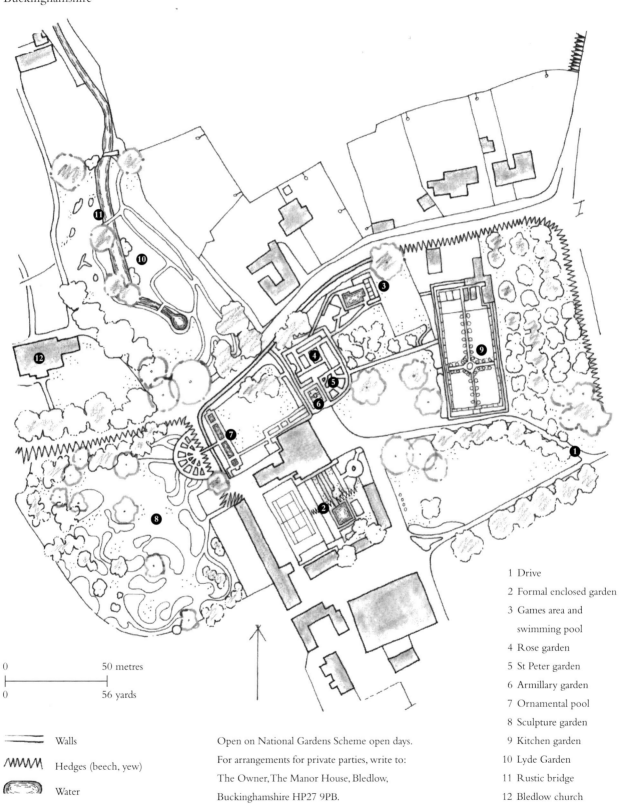

0   50 metres
├─────────────────┤
0   56 yards

≈≈≈≈≈ Walls

ʌʌʌʌʌ Hedges (beech, yew)

◉ Water

Open on National Gardens Scheme open days.
For arrangements for private parties, write to:
The Owner, The Manor House, Bledlow,
Buckinghamshire HP27 9PB.

1 Drive
2 Formal enclosed garden
3 Games area and
   swimming pool
4 Rose garden
5 St Peter garden
6 Armillary garden
7 Ornamental pool
8 Sculpture garden
9 Kitchen garden
10 Lyde Garden
11 Rustic bridge
12 Bledlow church

Chilcombe House
Chilcombe
Dorset

Open June: Wednesday (2–6).

1 Drive
2 Meadow
3 House
4 Borders
5 Lawn
6 Fountain
7 Terraced lawn and borders
8 Main axis
9 Pergola
10 Sundial
11 Orchard
12 Potager (including herbs)
13 Barn
14 Swimming pool
15 Vegetable garden
16 Paddock
17 Barn
18 Church
19 Farmyard
20 Ice house
21 Fernery
22 Shelter belt trees

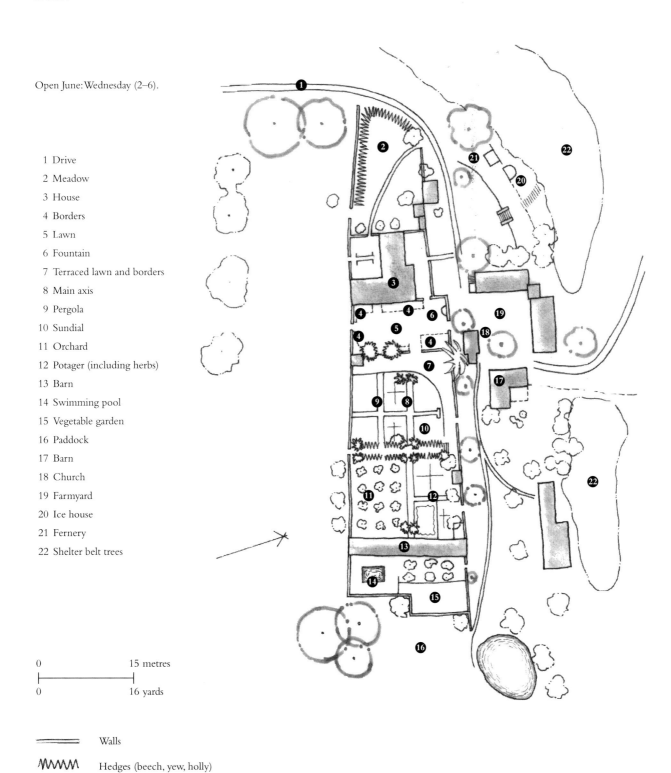

0   15 metres
0   16 yards

——— Walls

WWWW Hedges (beech, yew, holly)

▭ Water

Folly Farm
Sulhamstead
Berkshire

Open (garden only) mid-April to end
June on National Gardens Scheme
open days.
For private visits (all year round;
Tuesday, Wednesday, Thursday), write to:
The Owner, Folly Farm, Sulhamstead,
Berkshire RG7 4DF.

1 Orchard
2 Entrance court
3 Barn court
4 White garden
5 Canal garden
6 Flower parterre
7 Tank cloister
8 Sunken rose garden
9 Swimming pool
10 Lawn (rough grass area)
11 Kitchen garden

Garden area approx.
1.2 hectares (3 acres)

 Walls

 Hedges (yew)

 Water

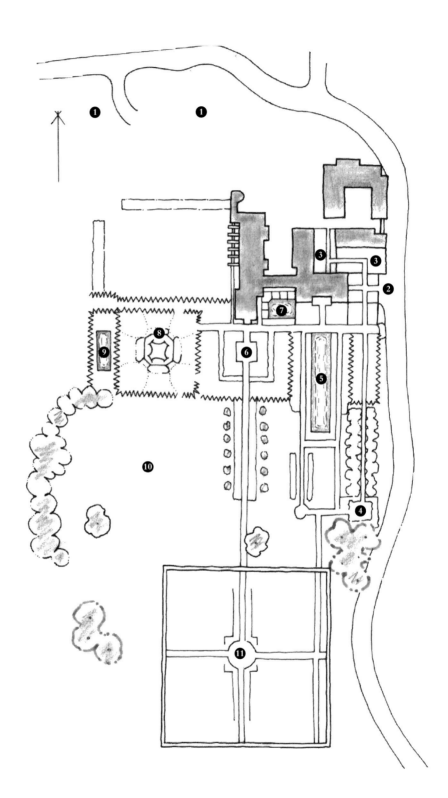

Great Dixter
Northiam
Sussex

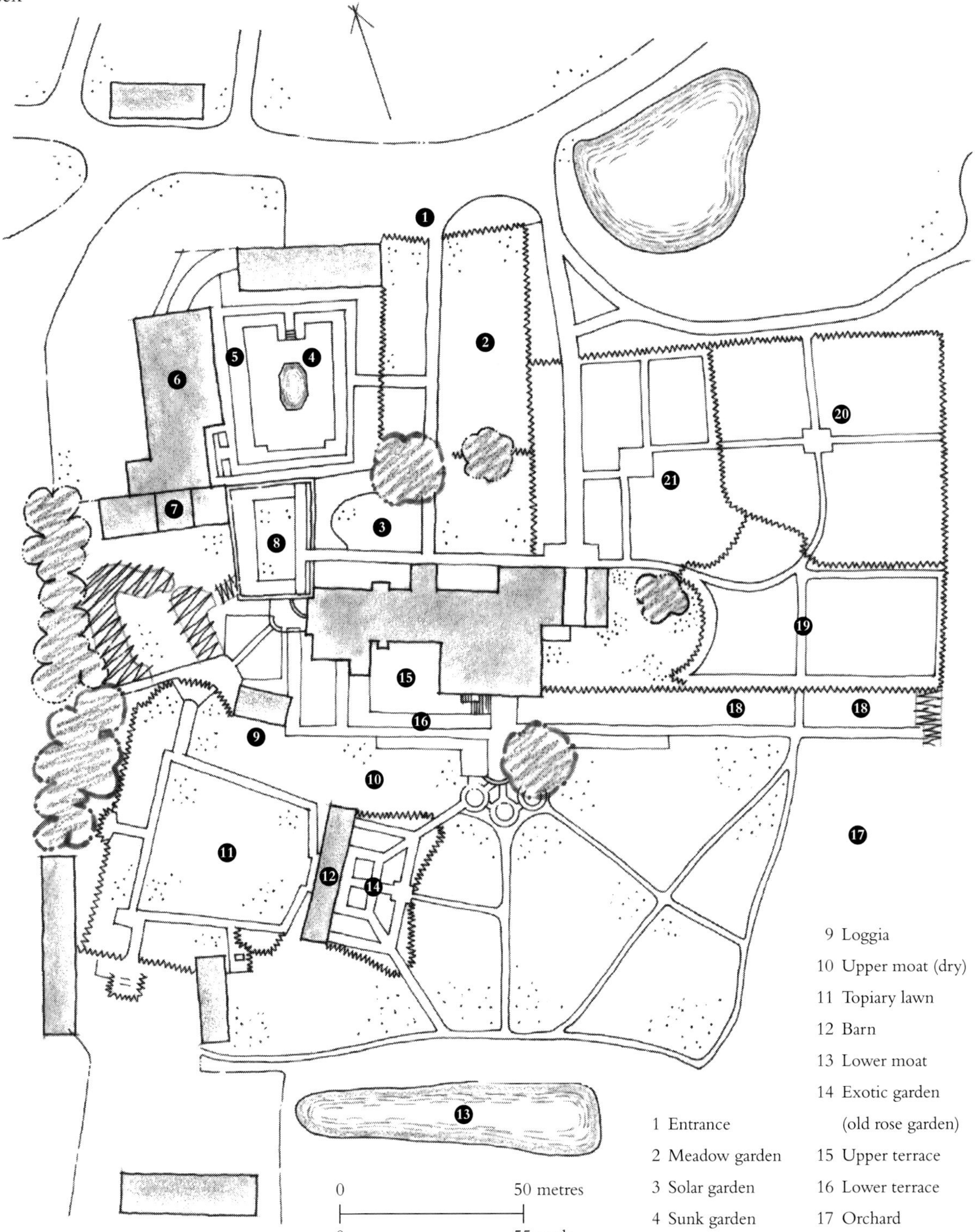

Open mid-April to October:
Monday to Sunday (9–12.30; 1.30–5).

0   50 metres

0   55 yards

∧∧∧∧∧   Hedges (yew/ilex)

    Water

1   Entrance
2   Meadow garden
3   Solar garden
4   Sunk garden
5   Barn garden
6   Barn
7   Oast house
8   Wall garden
9   Loggia
10   Upper moat (dry)
11   Topiary lawn
12   Barn
13   Lower moat
14   Exotic garden
     (old rose garden)
15   Upper terrace
16   Lower terrace
17   Orchard
18   Long border
19   Orchard garden
20   High garden
21   Peacock topiary

The Grove
Brightwell Baldwin
Oxfordshire

Garden open on written
applications to:
The Owner, The Grove,
Brightwell Baldwin,
Oxfordshire OX9 5PF

1 Drive
2 Mown lawn
3 Long grass
4 Magnolia room
5 See-through fence and gate
6 'Gothic tent'
7 Hornbeam room and statue
  of discus thrower
8 Double nut walk
9 Red room
10 Green room
11 Canal
12 Pavilion
13 Bridge
14 Secret garden
15 Pot terrace
16 Swimming pool
17 Horse chestnut avenue
18 Tennis court
19 Pond garden
20 Back drive

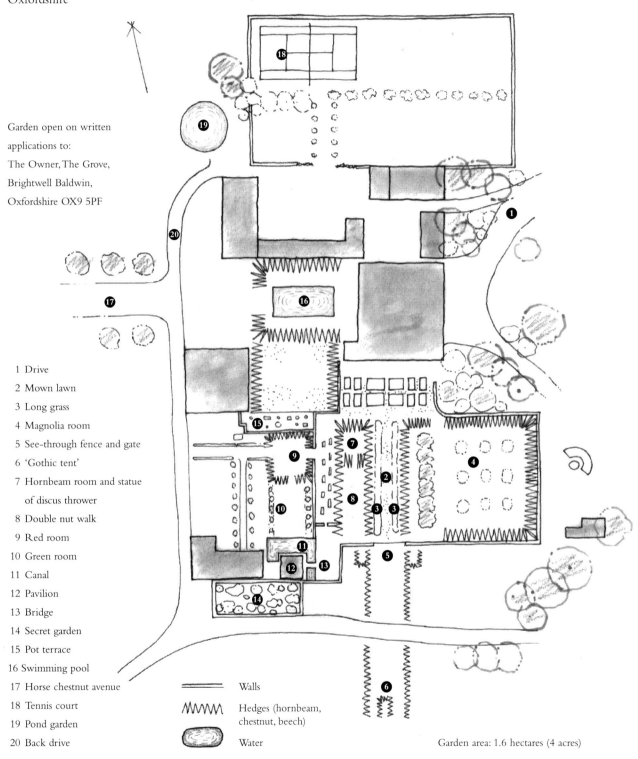

——————— Walls

WWWWW Hedges (hornbeam,
        chestnut, beech)

◯ Water

Garden area: 1.6 hectares (4 acres)

186

Helmingham Hall
Helmingham
Suffolk

Open end April to beginning September:
Sunday (2–6); Wednesday afternoons, by
appointment, for groups.

1 Garden entrance

2 New rose garden

3 Knot gardens

4 Herb beds

5 Hybrid Musk roses

6 Parterre

7 Spring border

8 Walled (kitchen) garden

9 Apple walk

10 Orchard garden

Garden area: approx. 4 hectares (10 acres)

 Walls

 Hedges (yew)

 Water

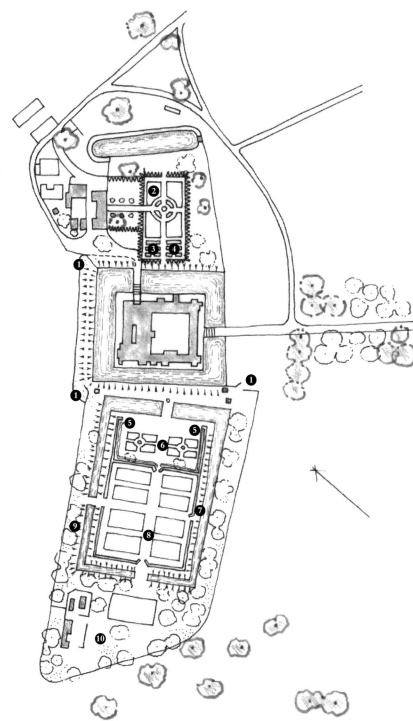

Holker Hall
Cark-in-Cartmel
Cumbria

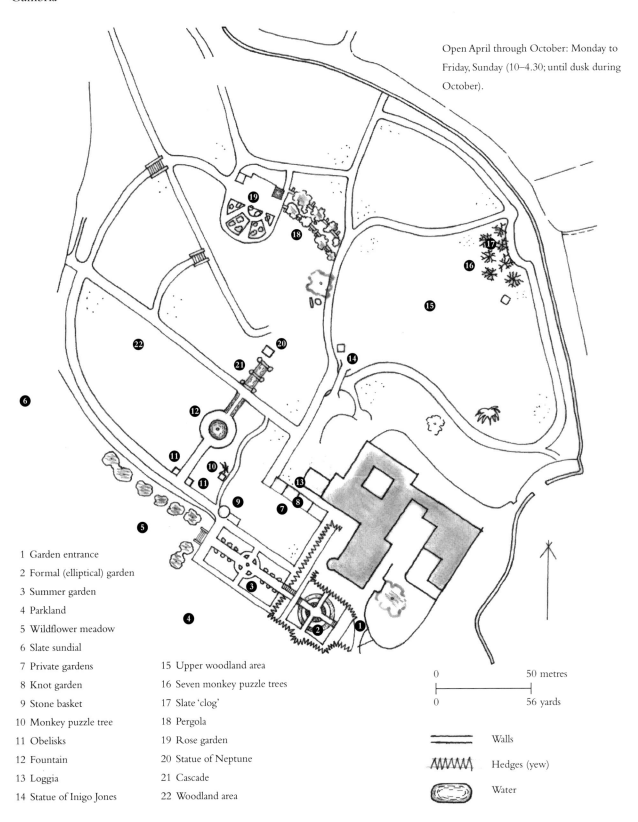

Open April through October: Monday to Friday, Sunday (10–4.30; until dusk during October).

1 Garden entrance
2 Formal (elliptical) garden
3 Summer garden
4 Parkland
5 Wildflower meadow
6 Slate sundial
7 Private gardens
8 Knot garden
9 Stone basket
10 Monkey puzzle tree
11 Obelisks
12 Fountain
13 Loggia
14 Statue of Inigo Jones
15 Upper woodland area
16 Seven monkey puzzle trees
17 Slate 'clog'
18 Pergola
19 Rose garden
20 Statue of Neptune
21 Cascade
22 Woodland area

0   50 metres
0   56 yards

——— Walls

WWWWW Hedges (yew)

Water

Kiftsgate Court
Chipping Campden
Gloucestershire

1 Four squares (paved garden)
2 White (sunken) garden
3 Bridge border
4 Kiftsgate rose
5 Rose border
6 Path edged with Rosa gallica
   'Versicolor'
7 Tennis court
8 Yellow border
9 Borders (north and south)
10 Terrace
11 Pine trees
12 Banks
13 Middle banks
14 Summer-house
15 Lower garden
16 Swimming pool
17 Ha-ha
18 Bluebell wood
19 Drive
20 Lily pond

Open April, May, August, September:
Wednesday, Thursday, Sunday, bank holiday
Mondays (2–6). June, July: Wednesday,
Thursday, Saturday, Sunday (12–6).

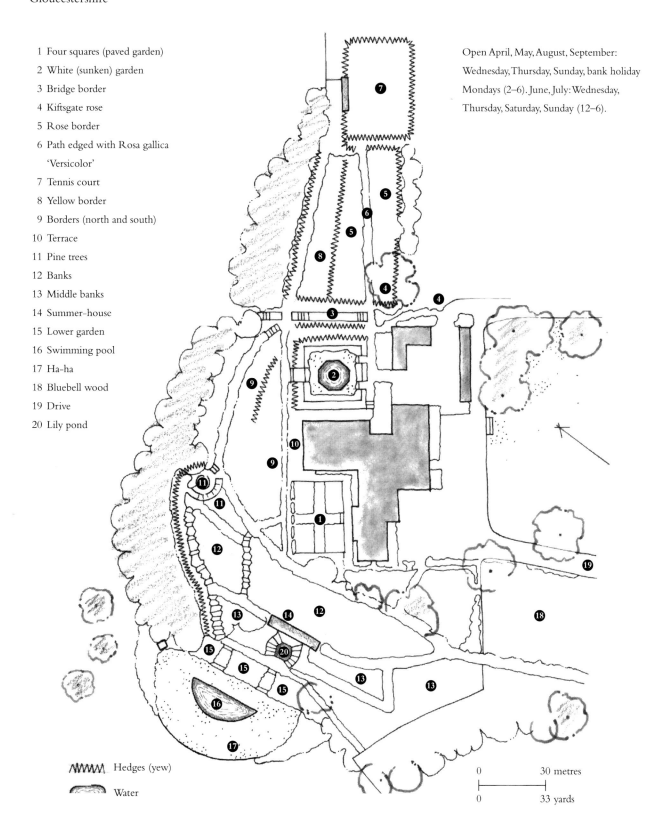

〰〰〰〰 Hedges (yew)

 Water

0   30 metres
├────────────────┤
0   33 yards

INDEX

This index lists plants and garden features in the book. Page numbers in *italic* refer to captions.